The Reminiscences

of

Chief Machinist's Mate
William Badders
U.S. Navy (Retired)

U.S. Naval Institute
Annapolis, Maryland
1986

Preface

As he brought out the first nine crew members of the 18 he was to rescue from the sunken submarine *Squalus* (SS-192) in May of 1939, Chief Machinist's Mate William Badders, USN (Ret.) says his first thought was for the *S-4* (SS-108). He lamented the fact that the equipment he was using hadn't been available to save the six men who initially survived the sinking of the *S-4* 11 and a half years earlier, but perished because there was no known way to get them out. His aggressive and courageous rescue of the *Squalus* crew members earned Badders a Medal of Honor from President Franklin D. Roosevelt, and his selfless thought at the time of the rescue gives an indication of this man who had risked his life in the line of duty several times before. In his oral history Chief Badders gives his first-hand account of the rescue and salvage efforts on the *Squalus*, the *S-4*, and the *S-51* (SS-162) lost in September 1925.

When Badders embarked on diving and salvage work in the mid-1920s, he was joining a community that was woefully underbudgeted, undermanned, and undertrained. From 1927 when the Navy finally established a full-time diving program at the Naval Gun Factory in Washington, D.C., Badders was at the forefront of experimental and practical diving and salvage in the United States. He was also a pioneer in underwater welding techniques and equipment in the mid-1930s.

But life was not all work for the athletic Badders. He played on the Pensacola Naval Air Station baseball team in the early 1920s that was one of the first teams to utilize air transportation to enlarge its circle of competition. During a 1921 cruise to Europe in the Kansas (BB-21), the crew put on non-stop exhibition baseball games for Norwegian fans. In the mid-1920s he played on the semiprofessional football team of the station ship Reina Mercedes (IX-25) at the Naval Academy. On the Asiatic Station serving in the Pigeon (AM-47) in the early 1930s, he was a contracted professional baseball player for a team in Manila where he went up against touring American pros Lou Gehrig and Satchel Paige. An injury with the Manila team sidelined Badders to coaching and managing the Holland (AS-3) team in the mid-1930s when they played against baseball great Ted Williams's high school team.

In 1940, Badders retired from active duty to take the position of master diver-salvage master for the Panama Canal, which was in the same backward state, as far as diving goes, that the Navy had been in 15 years before. Badders set up an organization, including a diving school, that kept the canal functioning for the 23 years that he held the job. One of the interesting incidents he recalls from that period was the salvaging of Anastasio Somoza's yacht, and the Nicaraguan President's kindness and generosity in return.

This finished volume is a tribute to Chief Badders's patience and to Dr. John T. Mason, Jr., former director of oral history, who conducted the interviews in 1971. The smooth typing was done by Mrs. Deborah Reid.

                                                        Susan B. Sweeney
                                                        Oral History Department
                                                        U.S. Naval Institute
                                                        July 1986

Chief Machinist's Mate William Badders, USN (Ret.)

Chief William Badders was born in Harrisburg, Illinois, on 15 September 1900, the son of George W. Badders and Sarah Martin Badders. He attended Rose Poly High School in Terre Haute, Indiana. During World War I he enlisted at Indianapolis and was sworn in as an apprentice seaman on 13 August 1918. Following boot training at the Great Lakes Naval Training Center, Badders was sent to Pensacola where he performed squadron maintenance. He served as an engineer in the battleship Kansas (BB-21) in 1921 and in the station ship Reina Mercedes (IX-25) at the Naval Academy from 1921 to 1924. During engineering duty in the salvage ship Falcon (ARS-2) from 1924 to 1926, Badders assisted in the salvage of the USS S-51 (SS-162), for which he received the Navy Cross. In August 1926 when he received this decoration, he also was promoted to chief machinist's mate. From 1926 to 1927 he was back in the Reina Mercedes and played on that ship's semiprofessional football team. Badders returned to the Falcon between 1927 and 1928 and took part in that ship's futile attempt to rescue crew members from the sunken S-4 (SS-108) in December 1927. He was tapped to be first a student and then an instructor at the newly-organized Navy Diving School in Washington, D.C., and in 1930 he returned to the Falcon for a third tour, this time as the ship's master diver. In 1931 he was master diver in the Pigeon (AM-47) on the Asiatic Station and played professional baseball in Manila. He returned to the United States in 1933 and served as master diver in the submarine tender Holland (AS-3) until 1936.

During his final active duty tour at the Experimental Diving Unit at the Naval Gun Factory in Washington, D.C., Badders was rushed to the site where the USS Squalus (SS-192) had sunk in 242 feet of water off Portsmouth, New Hampshire, in May of 1939. For his dangerous role in the rescue of 33 crew members from this submarine, Badders was awarded the Medal of Honor in January 1940 from President Roosevelt.

In 1940 he went to the Panama Canal as master diver-salvage master in an inactive duty status. He remained in that position until 1962 when he was mandatorily retired at the age of 62.

Badders has been married since 18 November 1922 to the former Lavinia Emma Tydings of Annapolis. They have a daughter, Beverly Marie Badders Roberts, and a son, Albert William Badders.

Authorization

The U.S. Naval Institute is hereby authorized to make available to individuals, libraries and other repositories of its choosing the transcripts of three oral history interviews concerning the life and career of the undersigned. The interviews were recorded on 14 and 22 September and 8 November 1971 in collaboration with John T. Mason, Jr., for the U.S. Naval Institute.

The undersigned does hereby release and assign to the U.S. Naval Institute all right, title, restriction, and interest in the interviews. The copyright in both the oral and transcribed versions shall be the sole property of the U.S. Naval Institute. The tape recordings of the interviews are and will remain the property of the U.S. Naval Institute.

Signed and sealed this ___14___ day of ___June___ 1986.

William Badders
Chief Machinist's Mate
U.S. Navy (Retired)

Interview Number 1 with Chief Machinist's Mate William Badders,
U.S. Navy (Retired)

Place: Chief Badders's home in Riva Woods, Annapolis, Maryland

Date: Tuesday morning, 14 September 1971

Subject: Biography

Interviewer: John T. Mason, Jr.

Q: It's certainly good to meet you, Mr. Badders. Bill Searle has been telling me a great deal about you and about your exciting career.* Would you tell me about your first contact with the Navy and your enlistment, how you happened to do this?

Chief Badders: Well, of course, this was in 1918 when World War I was going and I was the proper age to go in the service, so I went to Indianapolis. My home was Terre Haute, Indiana; they had a recruiting station there. Then I went through Indianapolis and was sworn in as an apprentice seaman on August 13, 1918. I was sent to Great Lakes training station for boot training. At the boot training, they lined about 300 or 400 of us up in ranks out on a big parade field, open ranks, and a couple of men walked through the ranks, looked you over and felt your muscle, and if you were healthy looking he'd have you fall out and fall into another company front. When it was all over, we had suddenly

---

*Captain Willard F. Searle, Jr., USN(Ret.), a salvage expert, is the subject of an as-yet-unpublished oral history that will eventually join the Naval Institute's collection.

Badders #1 - 2

become third class firemen instead of apprentice seamen. We were going to be in the engineering branch of the Navy.

Q: You weren't consulted; you were just inspected and sent there?

Chief Badders: They figured we had muscle enough to do the job and would grow up in it, and that was it.

Then we left Great Lakes, 300 or 400 of us in a group, and went to Norfolk to a receiving ship, and from there we were sent in groups to a squadron of ships that was operating in the Atlantic. I was sent aboard the old coal-burning battleship USS Wisconsin. About 25 of us went aboard that particular ship. When we got aboard with our bags and hammocks and all our paraphernalia and were put up on the forecastle and told to sit down and wait a while; there were some people coming around with some forms for us to fill out. Before we got started on that, one of the old-timers--he looked to me to be an old-timer at that time--on the ship came over to me and said, "Hey, kid, you don't want to shovel coal on this ship, do you?"

And I said, "Well, no, not if I can help it."

He said, "Okay, when you fill that form out, you tell them that you took a lot of mechanical training in high school, manual training, that you're mechanically inclined and all that."

I said, "Maybe that isn't just true."

He said, "Nobody's going to check it, and that may get you out of the fireroom and get you a better job." Then he walked off.

So I filled the form out in that vein and, sure enough, when they began to assign us to different divisions on the ship I was assigned to the engine room division. I stood watches in the engine room instead of shoveling coal, and I found out later that was the greatest thing that ever happened to me because the fellows shoveling coal on that ship really had to work.

Q: Yes, I've read stories of shoveling coal on battleships.

Chief Badders: So I stood watches in the engine room. At first, about all I did was wipe up the oil off the floor plates and things of that kind. Later I became kind of an oiler and just a general handyman on the shifts learning as much as I could, and I became really interested in the engineering.

We cruised around the Atlantic, short patrol runs that got us in the war zone—what was determined as a war zone at that time—which made me eligible for the World War I Victory Medal, Atlantic Fleet. We didn't really know when the armistice was signed. It was a surprise to us. I guess some people on the ship knew it, but the crew generally didn't know it. There was no excitement or anything on the ship. I heard later that other ships had big celebrations and all that, but on the old _Wisconsin_

Badders #1 - 4

we did nothing. I don't even remember where she was on November 11, 1918—moving around the Atlantic somewhere.

Then we came back in to Norfolk, and I was transferred back to Great Lakes Training Station in March of 1919. In December I did various things at the training station, mostly playing baseball and things of that kind to keep out of work. I became interested in aviation and put in for the aviation mechanics school at Great Lakes.

Q: You were not like a lot of them who had the urge to get out of the service?

Chief Badders: No, I didn't at that time. A little later that comes up, but at that time I had a four-year cruise to do, and I figured that was it and I was going to have to do it. So I figured aviation was coming along and I'd try to get in that branch. Well, I didn't make the school for some reason. I never did know why, but they did send me to the Naval Air Station at Pensacola. By this time, I was a fireman second class.

At Pensacola I did various things, mostly squadron work, waterfront work, pulling planes in and out of the water. They were all seaplanes there then. They didn't have planes with wheels on them in the Navy, not around there anyway. I played football with the naval air station football team and baseball, and we had the first football team that ever was transported by air. We flew out of Pensacola and went to Mobile, Alabama, and played Spring Hill College, the first time we ever flew, and from then on we flew most places we went away from the station to play. Then we did the same thing with the baseball team. We were quite proud of the fact that we'd pull into these towns with a couple of big old F-5L seaplanes with a football team aboard. Got a lot of publicity for the game!

Q: Give me a picture of Pensacola in those days.

Chief Badders: Well, they had two branches of aviation there. They had what we called heavier-than-air and lighter-than-air. Over in lighter-than-air were blimps and free balloons and the observation type balloon. We had a couple of old Eagle boats with winches on their fantail that would go out in the bay and release these observation balloons, and they'd go up in the air.* What they did up there I have no idea. But the blimps were real active. They flew all around the country down there. And then they had a lot of free ballooning, and they would ask for volunteers to go on these free-balloon hops. They'd take off from Pensacola with as many men in the basket as they could get

---

*Eagle-class patrol craft (PE), named from a 1918 <u>Washington Post</u> editorial calling for "...an eagle to scour the seas and pounce on every German submarine," were the result of the first American attempt to mass-produce ships. These 200-foot escort craft never made it into service during World War I and were of questionable quality, but many of the 60 ships built were used after the war as aircraft tenders.

in, and the first time it hit the ground, they drew lots for which one was going to drop out first, and when we hit the ground one would get out and, of course, that would relieve the ballast and make it go up and maybe travel some more, and so on down the line until the last two men were in and they used their regular sand ballast to go as far as they could. The last two men when they finally landed would have to make up the balloon and get back to the air station. Some of them got quite a distance away from the station.

Finally we had a disaster there. One of the balloons got in a cross current somehow and went to sea and there were about 12 men in it---10 men, I guess. We never did hear or see any more of them. That kind of knocked the free balloon on the head.

No one flew with parachutes, except the lighter-than-air people. I think they had some parachutes on the blimps, but over in heavier-than-air, where I was, we had three or four types of planes but nobody fooled with parachutes over there.

Q: Why not?

Chief Badders: Well, I guess they had them, but they just weren't issued. No one cared about them.

While I was there, Read came in with the NC-4 after his trip across the Atlantic with his crew, and that was quite a big thing around the station for a long time.* That crew of men who made that trip made history at the time.

We had quite a football team at Pensacola. Some of the young college grads who were going through flight training and the enlisted men played all over that part of the country. I had a very pleasant tour of duty, but for some reason or other in March of 1921 I found myself on a draft heading for Key West, Florida, in regular service. I had never got my rate changed from regular service to aviation and I, being a kid and not knowing any different, I should have looked into that before, but it never dawned on me that I should have done that.

When I got to Key West, I found out that we were going aboard another coal-burning battleship, the old USS Kansas. But by this time I'd smartened up enough to look out for myself when I got aboard her. The same thing, when you got aboard you had to fill out a form about your past experience, your qualifications, and things of that kind, so I filled out another form that I had been in motorboats around a naval air station, which I had, and that I had some experience in aviation engines and things like that. That application got me into the motorboat division, engineering motorboats, and I ended up as engineer of the admiral's barge,

---

*In May 1919 three Navy-Curtiss (NC) flying boats attempted a transatlantic flight from New York. Only NC-4, piloted by Lieutenant Commander Albert C. Read, USN, was successful, eventually making it to Portugal via the Azores.

old Admiral Hughes.*

    This <u>Kansas</u> was part of a fleet that came to the Naval Academy in June of 1921 and picked the midshipmen up for a midshipmen's cruise. That was one of the highlights of my seagoing career. We went from here, from the Academy, to what was at that time Christiania, Norway, now Oslo, and from there we went to Lisbon, Portugal, Gibraltar, Guantanamo Bay for a big exercise and all. Each ship had a baseball team. We used to play baseball among ourselves in port to get away if we had time enough. When we got to Christiania--I'll refer to it as Christiania because that's what it was at that time--the ambassador asked the admiral to send baseball teams ashore and play baseball for the benefit of the people because they had never seen American baseball. The time we were there, it was in the summer, of course, it never gets dark. It's daylight 24 hours a day, and we played baseball around the clock. I played 28 games of baseball in 14 days, and the only break between games was so that they could get one crowd out of the stadium and let another crowd in. We lived right at the stadium. They brought our food to us, and we stayed right there, so I didn't get to see much of Norway.

---

    *Rear Admiral Charles F. Hughes, USN, Commander Battleship Division Three and Battleship Squadron Two, Atlantic Fleet, in 1921. Admiral Hughes later served as Commander in Chief U.S. Fleet and still later as Chief of Naval Operations.

Q: It would take the pleasure out of playing baseball, wouldn't it?

Chief Badders: It sure did. We tried to have some of their athletes mix in with us to play the game with us, three or four on different teams as we played along, but they didn't pick up much in the short time we were there. They enjoyed it and they enjoyed watching us. The stadium wasn't big enough for baseball. It was really a soccer stadium, and we had to have all kinds of ground rules. When you hit a ball that would have been an easy out, it would be a home run. It'd be out of the park there.

During this midshipman's cruise I got very well acquainted with several of the midshipmen and I became interested in the Naval Academy, not to come here as a midshipman but for duty around here. I was told about all the boats they had at the Academy and all the athletics and all that business, and I thought, "Gee, that's the place for me to finish up my enlistment."

So, when we got back from the cruise, the Kansas was ordered out of commission. We got her put out of commission in December, and one of the rewards for doing a good job in putting the ship out of commission and all this is that they give the crew a preference of where they want the duty from that duty station. They would give them as near what they wanted as they could. Well, there were eight or ten of us on the ship who put in for

Badders #1 - 10

duty here at the old Reina Mercedes and we arrived here.* We got it. I came to the Reina Mercedes on December 31, 1921 and did an enjoyable tour of duty here.

Q: What were your duties?

Chief Badders: by this time I was a second class engineman mate. I made first class fireman on the Kansas. Then about the time I was transferred to the Reina Mercedes, I made second class engineman.

I went to work in the engineering branch on the old Reina down at the boathouse. The boathouse was down on the waterfront where some of the new Bancroft Hall is now; that street that runs behind the new Bancroft Hall was the waterfront street at that time. The boathouse was down at what had been a pier that went out to where the old Reina Mercedes was tied up. I operated the crew coach's boat for two years, and that was enjoyable work, but, of course, that was only part of the year. I went to Poughkeepsie with the crews. Dick Glendon was the head coach at the time I was operating the boat.** He had relieved his father,

---

*The USS Reina Mercedes (IX-25) had originally been an unprotected cruiser in the Spanish Navy. She was captured by the United States in the Spanish-American War of 1898. She served as station ship at Annapolis from 1912 to 1957.
**Richard J. "Young Dick" Glendon, Jr., was a crew coach at the Naval Academy from 1919 to 1925. His father, "Old Dick," coached crew from 1903 until 1922.

and they were quite famous crew coaches. Young Dick was very temperamental and scared the pants off me one time. We'd been up the Severn River for a workout and coming back the crew had gone way ahead of us, and I wasn't paying much attention. The coach had got out of the front cockpit and had moved to the back of the boat. I wasn't paying any attention to him back there. I was watching the crews to make sure I didn't run into any shell's oars or anything, and when I got close to the old boathouse, which was right across the street from the drill field down there at the time, I didn't have any coach in the back of the boat. Nobody in the boat but me!

I couldn't imagine what had happened, so instead of making a landing I turned around and went back as hard as I could go, retracing my steps almost to the railroad bridge, and here's Dick Glendon swimming. I went over to try and pick him up and he ran me off. He said, "Get away from here, I'm swimming back." Well, that was still a long swim he had, and when he went overboard I really don't know—somewhere around the old railroad bridge. I stayed behind him and kept along with him all the way back anyway, although he kept hollering at me to get away from him and let him alone. I don't know yet why he jumped overboard at that point. I think he was a little disappointed with the workout or something.

In 1924 they brought the alumni crew back to the Academy that had won the Olympics in 1920, Frawley and everybody in the crew except the stroke they had that stroked the crew in 1920, a man by the name of King.* For some reason he didn't come back. I don't know what the reason was. But they had the original coxswain and the whole crew, and they worked out for a couple of months down at the Academy. Old man Glendon came back to coach them. They were going to represent the Navy in the Olympics if they could. We went to Philadelphia for the tryouts, and they had wonderful time trials down the Severn River, and the Navy varsity shell crew at that time was great, too. We were so sure that the alumni crew was going to beat everything in the Olympic trials that they even had a cruiser ready to take the shells and the men, me, and the coach boat and everything to Paris; the Olympics were in Paris. Well, it turned out that we didn't win. Yale beat the alumni crew, and our two Navy crews came in second and third. The alumni crew—some of them were officers and some were civilians—beat the midshipmen by a quarter of a boat's length of something.

Anyway, we didn't get our trip to Paris. Instead of going to Paris, we came back to the Academy.

During this tour of duty on the Reina Mercedes I served under

---

*The crew team from the Naval Academy that won the gold medal at the 1920 summer Olympics at Antwerp consisted of Midshipmen Virgil V. Jacomini '21A, Edwin D. Graves, Jr. '21A (captain), William C. Jordan '22, Edward P. Moore '21B, Alden R. Sanborn '22, Donald H. Johnston '22, Vincent J. Gallagher, Jr. `22, Clyde W. King '22, and Sherman R. Clarke '22. Midshipman Edward R. Frawley '22 rowed on the second varsity team, but was not a member of the Olympic squad.

Badders #1 - 13

Abram Claude, a famous name here in Annapolis, Captain Claude, and his executive officer was Henry Hartley, a lieutenant.* I got very well acquainted with Hartley, and his tour of duty was up about the same time mine was here. He told me that he was going to the only salvage ship that the Navy had, the old USS Falcon, and he would like for me to go along as the salvage ship had a lot of salvage equipment aboard, gasoline engine driven pumps, and things of that kind, and he thought I would maybe like that type of work.

Q: This meant that you had to reenlist?

Chief Badders: Yes, I had reenlisted. In October of 1924 I left the Reina Mercedes. By this time I was an engineman first class. I went aboard the Falcon in the Brooklyn Navy Yard, and I never was so sorry for asking for anything in my life as I was when I saw the condition of that thing. She was just a glorified tug, actually a minesweeper converted, and she had a recompression chamber aboard and an air system and a lot of

---

*Captain Claude's first American ancestor, also named Abram, came to Annapolis from Switzerland prior to the American Revolution, and distinguished himself as an aggressive resister to the Stamp Act. Among his descendents have been an Annapolis mayor, state treasurer, and various physicians and military officers.

salvage equipment.* But that was the dirtiest, hottest, most disorganized ship I've ever seen in my life. I hadn't seen very many, but I knew what a ship should look like. And I thought, "Oh, boy, I'm going to get away from this thing just as soon as I possibly can."

Of course, a big lot of this trouble was the fact that she was in the navy yard for an overhaul and she was all torn apart. But, of course, I had to go aboard and report in and I was put in the engine room. The engineering department, the interim crew, was doing about 50% of the overhaul themselves. They were working like Trojans. Hartley didn't get to the ship for quite some time, and I began to worry that he wasn't going to get there. I knew if he ever got to the ship there'd be some changes made, because he wasn't going to put up with anything as lousy as that. The crew was a helter-skelter bunch of people, no discipline. Uniform wasn't heard of—you'd see them in white hats, but overalls instead of regular dungarees. Oh, it was a disorganized piece of Navy equipment.

Sure enough, Hartley finally came aboard. They had a little change-of-command ceremony, and he waited until the man he relieved got off the ship, kept the crew at quarters back on the fantail—there were only about 65 men on this thing—and he gave

---

*The USS _Falcon_ was commissioned as a minesweeper in November 1918 and served in a variety of roles thereafter. She was officially reclassified a submarine rescue ship, ASR-2, on 12 September 1929. With a displacement of 950 tons, the _Falcon_ was 187 feet 10 inches long and 35 feet 6 inches in the beam.

them a little talking-to.

Q: He had inspected the ship?

Chief Badders: Yes, and he said the same thing that I had thought when I saw the ship. He said he had never seen such a disorganized, dirty ship as the one that he had just taken over, and that he would not tolerate any such conditions; changes had to be made. He said, "We'll make them gradually, and I'm sure you people will be proud of the results, and we'll see what we can do with this." And, sure enough, before we got out of the navy yard, by the time they began to put the ship back together he had enforced some regulations about uniforms and the food, the chow and the service, and things of that kind, the stowage of clothing, the bunks, and the quarters, and all, and it began to look like a place for Navy men. The crew did start to become interested in keeping the ship up.

We left the navy yard and went to New London, Connecticut; the Falcon was part of the old Control Force, the submarines and the submarine tenders: the Bushnell, Camden, Savannah, and the Falcon. We made a cruise from New London, and the Falcon was getting to be more like a Navy ship all the time, and by the time we got back to the navy yard for another overhaul, that was some time late in 1925, she was really a nice-looking ship and a joy to be aboard.

As I say, we were in the navy yard in 1925 for a minor overhaul. The ship had had some main engine problems, and finally the main engine was up in the shops and one evening—I don't remember the date now—we got word that a submarine had been sunk outside of Newport, just off Block Island, and for the Falcon to get there with her equipment and any divers she had aboard as soon as she could.* Admiral Plunkett was commandant of the Brooklyn Navy Yard at the time and he called the workmen in and they threw that ship together like nothing's ever been put together before.** By the next day at noon we were under way with navy yard workmen swarming all over the ship even yet. They followed them with motorboats and as one workman would finish his job he'd get in the boat, get a boat loaded, and get back to the Brooklyn Navy Yard.

As I said, this Falcon was a salvage ship, but she had no divers aboard at all. There wasn't a single diver aboard her. She didn't have a lot of equipment. Gasoline-driven pumps and air compressors and things of that kind, and she had a beautiful air system permanently installed in the ship with two big low-pressure air compressors in the firerooms and a big

---
*On the night of 25 September 1925, the USS S-51 (SS-162) was rammed and sunk off of Block Island, New York. Of the 36 men on board, only three survived. She was raised on 5 June 1926 and sold for scrap in June 1930.
**Rear Admiral Charles P. Plunkett, USN. The shipyard at Brooklyn was known officially as the New York Navy Yard. Plunkett was commandant of both the navy yard and the Third Naval District.

high-pressure system aboard, but no men who had done any underwater work.

Q: This had not been thought necessary?

Chief Badders: Hartley knew it was necessary, but the Navy just didn't have that kind of people then. They didn't have divers in the Navy that amounted to anything at all. Our only diving at that time that amounted to anything at all was around Newport, where they had a crew of divers whose main job was recovering lost torpedoes from the torpedo range, and they were diving 50, 60, 70, and sometimes as much as 100 feet out there. They were about the only divers we had. The only training facility they had for divers in the Navy then was the old seamen gunners school in Washington, D.C. They put men down 50 or 75 feet with a hand pump and put them on the bottom for 20 minutes, bring them up, and say, "Okay, you're a diver." That was it, and they might never make another dive unless they were on some ship that had diving equipment and got a propeller fouled or something or to look for something that dropped overboard, something of that nature.

When we arrived on the scene where the S-51 was down, by this time it had been determined there was no one alive in the boat.

Q: How deep was she?

Chief Badders: She was in about 132 feet of water, and the divers who were out there were the men from Newport Torpedo Station--Tom Eadie, Fred Michels, and Jimmy Ingram were the diving crew at the Newport Torpedo Station*. Ingram and Michels were in the Navy, both chief petty officers, and Tom Eadie had been in the Navy for 12 years or so and had quit and taken over the job as the diving boss at the torpedo station. They had been to the deck of the boat and pounded around on all the hatches and things and determined that there was no one alive at all, so there was no rescue operation involved here. It was strictly a salvage job. They brought cranes out from the Brooklyn Navy Yard and tried to lift her with cranes, but cranes in the open sea have never been any good, so we didn't accomplish anything.

Q: What had caused her to go down?

Chief Badders: She had been rammed by a commercial ship; the _City of Rome_ hit her and cut her almost in two. She was on what we called at that time a ten-day patrol run, running with lights out and all that business, and was on the surface when the _City of Rome_ hit her. The only men who got off of her were the men who were in the conning tower. It was at night, dark, of course, and the only men that got off were the men on watch in the

---

*Chief Gunner's Mate Thomas Eadie, USNRF; Chief Torpedoman Fred G. Michels, USN; Chief Torpedoman James C. Ingram, USN.

conning tower. I think one man, maybe, got out of the hatch before they got the hatches closed. Anyway, there were five men who got out of her, and three of those five were picked up by the lifeboat of the City of Rome and two others died in the water, waiting to be picked up. The three men who were picked up said they knew that time stretched out in a case of that kind, but they were fully convinced that they were in the water over an hour before the City of Rome put the lifeboat in the water and picked them up.

Evidently, the City of Rome didn't know what she had hit and didn't realize there were men in the water until finally they heard them holler or something.

Q: What was the City of Rome?

Chief Badders: She was a coastal ship plying mostly between Boston and New York, combination passenger and cargo.

Q: Similar to what the Ward Line used to have?

Chief Badders: Right.

Well, here were all these men inside the submarine, dead, and the parents of the people and wives and so on wanted these bodies recovered, so they decided they were going to salvage this submarine. Admiral Plunkett put a lieutenant commander in charge of the job. I guess he was famous before that, but he became famous after, Lieutenant Commander Edward Ellsberg, a famous name in the Navy later.* They started to work, first, trying to recover some of the bodies. They opened the hatches, put divers inside, and they recovered some of the bodies but couldn't get all of them. A lot of places they couldn't get to.

The system of raising a submarine was to use the Navy submarine pontoons, and seal off as many tanks as they could and get rid of as much water inside as they could to lighten the load as much as possible. What they couldn't lighten, they'd overcome with the pontoons. They worked until late in November. The weather was terrific. They worked one day and were off three, running for shelter to stop them from turning over themselves, ice cold, and the thing that made us finally have to stop altogether was that the divers' air hoses were beginning to freeze up. We almost lost a man. He was on the bottom, and his air was stopped all at once. We brought him to the surface and his air hose was full of a kind of frost.

---

*Lieutenant Commander Edward Ellsberg, USN, top man in the Naval Academy class of 1914, first came to prominence as salvage officer on the S-51 (SS-162) in 1926. He resigned from the Navy that same year, returning for reserve duty for two blocks of time and eventually retiring from the Naval Reserve as a rear admiral in 1951. He is best known as a prolific inventor in the oil industry and author of many books, including On the Bottom (New York: The Literary Guild of American, Inc., 1929), about his experiences with the S-51. The book contains a photo of some two dozen Navy divers who were involved in the salvage of the S-51.

Q: Condensation.

Chief Badders: Condensation that froze up in the hose. So they decided they'd quit until the warm weather.

The <u>Falcon</u> went back to New London, and we made a cruise to Panama with the submarines. We were supposed to take a bunch of young fellows, including myself, and start breaking them in as divers down in Panama, but we never did get around to that. We were too busy towing targets and towing submarines and things around for the submarine maneuvers. We never had a dive in the water. They had a grand total of six men on the job up to that time that were capable of making dives to the bottom. They were scattered all over the Navy, and they called them together for that particular job.

Q: Were you anxious to learn to be a diver?

Chief Badders: Oh, yes, I wanted to get right in the thick of things, but I didn't make out for quite a while.

We went back in the spring and went to work on the submarine and finally got her ready with all the pontoons down, and that became my job, rigging the pontoons and getting them ready to go down for the divers to work on them. That was quite a job at that time. The pontoons were not as modern as the ones we had later, and they were quite a thing to handle.

Q: How many were required?

Chief Badders: We used eight pontoons on the S-51.

Q: What was her tonnage?

Chief Badders: Each pontoon lifted 80 tons.

Q: What was the tonnage of the S-51?

Chief Badders: I don't remember, I'd have to look it up.* We got the thing all ready to blow and we were going to raise her in the morning. There were bad weather reports coming, and by morning it really was bad. Too choppy to attempt to bring the submarine to the surface, but we had a lot of leaks. You could see bubbles coming to the surface all around from some places in the pontoons and some from compartments and hatches that we had put in place. By this time I had made a dive or two.

So Ellsberg decided to go back in the morning, hook up some of the air hoses, and compensate for some of the loss of buoyancy that was in the tanks and pontoons, overcome some of these leaks. They hooked up to some of the bow pontoons and didn't blow more than a minute or two before there was a terrific commotion in the

---

*The USS S-51 displaced 1,230 tons submerged.

water almost right under the fantail of the *Falcon*. One man grabbed an axe and cut the mooring line leading out of the chocks on that side and let the *Falcon* swing free just in time, and up came the bow of the *S-51* with four pontoons. I have a picture of that right over there.

After this bow came up, Ellsberg decided to try to raise the stern anyway, regardless of the weather which was getting worse all the time. So they blew everything out they could and, with the bow up, put an angle on the boat because they couldn't get all the water out of the engine room that they had planned to get out due to the angle of the boat. So they went ahead and blew the after pontoons and the after pontoon chains broke and let that pair of pontoons come to the surface. Then they knew they couldn't raise her. Here she is beating herself to death up there and the pontoons are beating themselves to pieces, and the only thing to do to save her was to get her and the pontoons back on the bottom.

Sometime before that, they had closed off all the flood valves on the pontoons and they couldn't be flooded in the condition they were in to let them go back to the surface. Somebody had to get aboard the pontoons and open the flood valves so the pontoons would flood and let the bow go back, and that became my job. I volunteered, I guess. I could probably have refused to go, but . . .

Q: Kind of dangerous, wasn't it?

Chief Badders: Yes, because the seas were breaking together over the pontoons and they were banging together. If you got washed in between a pair of pontoons, why, you'd have had to be scraped off or something the next day or two. But you never thought of those things when something had to be done; you just went ahead and did it.

When we went back in the spring to work on the boat, Captain Ernie King, who was the commanding officer of the submarine base at New London, Connecticut, had become the overall officer in charge of the salvage operation.* I always have thought that was one of the only mistakes that Admiral King made—he was later Admiral King but I refer to him as admiral all the time. He made me put on a great big old kapok life jacket to go out on those pontoons with a line around me to a motorboat. Of course, when those seas hit me and I was on that pontoon with that big old kapok jacket on, I could hardly hang on. I'd have been able to hang on much better without the life jacket. He thought he was making it safer for me by putting me in a life jacket.

Anyway, I got enough of the valves open to flood enough of the pontoon to put the bow back on the bottom, and when the

---

*Captain Ernest J. King, USN, Commander in Chief U.S. Fleet during World War II, commanded the submarine base at New London, Connecticut, from 1923 to 1926.

weather calmed down we went to work again and cleared everything up. Some of the pontoons had to be brought to the surface, repaired, and put back down, but eventually we brought her to the surface and headed for the Brooklyn Navy Yard. We got within sight of the dry dock gate, and the pilot we had aboard to take her through Hell Gate ran her aground on what they called, and I guess still do, Man-o-War Rock out in the river. That created quite a problem. We had to shorten up the chains on the pontoons, let the pontoons down farther on the chains to get more lift to raise her off of this rock. That was accomplished with a lot of risk and work and some luck. While we were lowering the pontoons, we had a crane out there holding the chains up through the hawsepipes and we'd flood the pontoon down as far as we could and hold it there, then put the toggle bar back through the chain at that point. While one of these operations was going on, somebody got through the Coast Guard patrol that was out in the river keeping traffic away, went by and kicked up a swell and made the crane bob up and down and broke the sling that was holding one of the chains up, and it flew back down through the hawsepipe. It created quite a job getting the chain back up and holding the pontoon. I stood on the pontoon in water up to my neck, with my thumbs in the holes--I was actually on my knees, I wasn't standing--with my thumbs in the holes where we had taken valves off until we got some wooden plugs to plug them up until the valves could be replaced.

Anyway, finally we got everything all ready. The big rush on this was to get one of the highest tides they were going to have in the river for some long time. They wanted to catch it right at high tide and try to lift her off this rock. As it turned out, that's exactly what we did. We got this thing in dry dock, removed all the bodies and all that business. Then she was scrapped.

Well, from that work I did opening the valves on the pontoons and other work there and the work on the pontoons in the North River where she ran aground, I was recommended for and received from the President the Navy Cross. Commander Ellsberg and Hartley, when the S-51 job was completed, made many recommendations for changes aboard the submarines. For instance, the salvage air system that they had on the old S-boats, the R-boats, and the O-boats there was one fitting in the conning tower that a diver could hook a hose to and supposedly distribute air all through the submarine. Well, if that line got damaged anyplace in the boat, that's as far as the air went. Their recommendation was that there should be fittings on deck for air connections in every compartment and that some investigation should be made into the possibility of rescuing people from submarines in case anyone's alive when a submarine's on the bottom, and some changes in the construction of the pontoons. That was done. The changes in the pontoons were actually performed, but nothing else.

Q: What kind of changes were they?

Chief Badders: The old pontoons had only one bulkhead, in the center, which meant that when you opened the flood valves on the bottom of the thing to flood it, you had no way of controlling the amount of water you put in the pontoon, except turning the air off on the vent hose and closing the flood valves. When you get this thing heavy enough to sink itself with the water aboard, somebody had to close these valves, which meant that she was already underwater 6 or 8 feet. And that was another one of my jobs on the salvage operation, to get these flood valves closed. They were great big 12-inch gate valves that required 17 turns to close them, and that took a long time.

Q: And meanwhile she was going down?

Chief Badders: No. They were holding her as best they could at that point. As soon as it would go in the water, they'd turn the vent off and hold everything they had on the lowering lines, but it continued to take some water in compressing the air in the top, and it would be getting heavier all the time and putting strain on the lowering lines. It would get a little deeper—we'd have them, before I could get the valves closed, go down as much as 10 feet. I'd be on a diving stage over the side, lying on my stomach, turning a big key wrench, a big long, extended-handle key wrench to close the valves and I'd be under 10 feet of water before I could get them closed.

But the new alteration on the pontoons, they put two bulkheads in some of them and in some they put a buoyancy chamber in the center, which meant you could flood the two ends and keep the center compartment dry, and you could control the amount of water you put in the two ends and make the thing weigh any tonnage you wanted. On the *S-4* and *Squalus* jobs, we put the pontoons down weighing about eight tons, although we had to handle the lowering lines to put them down in place. That was about the only thing that was really accomplished out of all the recommendations that were made.

Another thing—Hartley, seeing the big need for divers in the Navy, wanted some means of training more divers and making the ones we had better divers.*

Q: Why did the Navy not have divers up to this point?

Chief Badders: They had no reason for them, they thought, up to then, I guess. They'd only had one submarine disaster and that was out in Honolulu in 1914. That was a little old F-boat out

---

*In an article in the March 1931 issue of the Naval Institute's *Proceedings* entitled "Some Historical Facts on Diving," pages 341-349, Lieutenant Hartley discusses improvements in diving techniques and equipment, the salvage operations on *S-51* and *S-4*, and the Navy's recruitment and training of divers.

there, and they picked her up by sweeping wires under her and bringing her in to shallow water, which required very little diving. They just hadn't had any need for divers.

Q: Had private enterprise had salvage . . .

Chief Badders: Yes. Merritt, Chapman, and Scott had their own divers, but there again I'd say 90% of their work was underwater construction work. It wasn't so much salvage, and a lot of their salvage work required very little diving. It was mostly groundings and things of that kind.

After the S-51 job was finished, I was discharged and reenlisted, and I came back to the Academy, to the old Reina Mercedes, supposedly for a football season. I played football with the old Reina Mercedes semipro team. We called it the Reina Mercedes. We had a few sailors playing, but we also played a lot of the assistant coaches, graduates of the Academy were assistant coaches, and we had quite a football team. We played all over the country.

Q: By that time you'd decided to make the Navy your career?

Chief Badders: Oh, yes. Right after I reenlisted, I found out that--in 1926 I became chief machinist's mate, part of that was due to my Navy Cross decoration.* I was on the list for chief. At that time you took examinations for chief, whatever your rate was, and you competed with the whole Navy. If you were on the list, according to the marks you made in the examination, and at the end of the year if you hadn't reached the top, the list was wiped out and you had to take another examination. I'd done that twice, made the list, but nowhere near the top but somewhere close to the top. It could have been another two or three years before I'd made it. It was part of my reward for the work we'd done--I wasn't the only one; there were three or four others in the same condition I was on the list, with different ratings, boatswain's mate, carpenter's mate. Ellsberg recommended that we be jumped off of the list to our chief grade. All of us made chief. I got chief a year or two ahead of time, ahead of what I would have normally.

During this football season, I got a knee torn up at the Academy and spent a lot of time in the hospital. I ended up being here almost a year. In fact, it was a year. In August of 1927, I went back to the Falcon, and after I was on the Falcon a short while, in 1928, the S-4, we learned, was on the bottom in New London, Connecticut. I was here in Annapolis on leave-- Christmas leave. The S-4 was rammed and sunk. She was hit by a

---

*Engineman first class Badders received the Navy Cross on 2 August 1926, signed by Chief of Naval Operations Admiral Edward W. Eberle, USN, as acting Secretary of the Navy for President Coolidge. Badders was on the list for chief, but the engineman rating was being phased out. When he received his citation he was jumped off the waiting list and rated chief machinist's mate.

Coast Guard patrol destroyer, what they called a rum-chaser. The S-4 was running the measured mile outside of Provincetown, Massachusetts, submerged, and the Coast Guard destroyer Paulding evidently didn't know she was in the area and ran through that measured mile area, slammed into her, and did enough damage to sink her.

On her there were six men alive in the forward torpedo room.

Q: How far down was she?

Chief Badders: She was down 102 feet. I was on leave here in Annapolis, and I went right down to the Reina Mercedes and told them I had to get back to the Falcon as soon as possible. By this time, I knew the Falcon was under way to Portsmouth. While I was there, Captain King came through there. How we got together I just don't remember, but anyway we caught a plane out of Annapolis somewhere. We went aboard a seaplane and flew to Boston, and from Boston we went to Provincetown and aboard the Falcon.

Well, here were these six men alive in the forward torpedo room and no way to save them, no way of getting them out of there. The divers had hooked up the salvage air hose to this conning tower arrangement that I mentioned was on the S-51, and when they turned the air on, it just squirted right out about 10 feet forward of the control tower at the end of the pipeline where it had been cut in two when the Paulding hit her. So there was no way of getting air into the forward torpedo room. The divers were doing different tasks on the bottom. Fred Michels got fouled up on the bottom. The seas were terrific, there was just a terrific blow, and that is one of the worst spots on the Atlantic Coast when it gets bad, right off the point of Provincetown. The Falcon was in a four-point mooring, and he had two big seagoing tugs over on her seaward side with lines running to her and trying to hold her up in the moorings so the divers could work on the bottom. She was yawing back and forth, as they tried to hold her steady, but they just couldn't do it.

Fred Michels got all fouled up on the bottom in the wreckage, part of the bow of the Paulding and part of the wreckage of the S-4 submarine. He couldn't get out of there, and Tom Eadie was put back down--he'd already made one dive that morning, but he was put back down to try to get Michels freed, which he did after an hour or two. By this time Michels had a very severe case of bends, and the Falcon was tearing up her mooring lines. It was just impossible to stay there and do anything, so they decided they would have to get out of there and they disconnected everything and left. And there were these six men aboard in the forward torpedo room, but nothing could be done. But the fact that the Navy had to leave so soon really put headlines in the papers about the Navy abandoning their men on the bottom of the ocean and all that kind of thing. Of course, the people who wrote these articles couldn't have been there and seen the conditions or they'd never have written them.

We got back as soon as we possibly could, got back on the moorings and sent divers down again. They were receiving taps, signals by hammer raps on the hull from the inside from these men for 30 hours, and after 30 hours they didn't receive any more, which indicated they had become unconscious and died shortly thereafter. By the time the Falcon got back on the moorings and got men down, it was an established fact that the men were by this time dead. Nothing could be done. So then this became strictly a salvage job, and here again we only had a very few divers, scattered all over the Navy. Myself and a man by the name of Frazer who had been on the S-51 job were the only two men in the Falcon's ship's company who had had any diving experience at all.* The other men had to be called in from all over, a couple from the Torpedo Station, Newport, and one from as far away as Honolulu came in. It was a month or more later before he got there. And we had even a civilian on the job. They put him in the Naval Reserve, a fellow by the name of Anderson, so they could use him as a diver.

Captain Savvy Saunders was the salvage officer in charge, and from all the experience we had on the S-51, the placing of the hatches and pontoons and all that kind of thing, was more or less

---

*Chief Torpedoman James W. Frazer, USN.

a repetition of what we had done on the S-51 job.* It was just a matter of doing again what had been done before. She was raised very successfully and put in the Boston Navy Yard dry dock.

In the meantime, while all this was going on, here were all these people raising all this commotion about the Navy letting these men die on the bottom, and Admiral Brumby, one of the finest old men that ever served—by the way, he was my commanding officer years before in the old battleship Kansas when he was a captain.** By this time he was rear admiral and commanding the Submarines Control Force. He was put on the pan terrifically because, being the big man in charge, he should have facilities to do things. Of course, anybody who knows anything about the Navy knows they can only do what they have the money to do with and the time to do it and so on. At that time we just weren't spending money for that type of business.

Anyway, before this job was finished, the politicians in Washington had decided, well, we're going to do something about this, and they gave them unlimited money and time and everything else to set up diving schools and buy equipment, experiment with equipment, and all this, and really get a salvage and rescue organization in the Navy. Well, when the job was over, the S-4 in dry dock and everything, by this time Captain King was in aviation. He had just finished his flight training at Pensacola

---

*Commander Harold E. Saunders, USN.
**Rear Admiral Frank H. Brumby, USN.

and he told me, "Look, you ought to get out of this general salvage and get into aviation."

And I said, "Well, admiral, I've got news for you. I was in aviation at one time and liked it very much, but I've never been able to get back in it."

He said, "Well, that's the thing to get into in the Navy now. Get out of this, it's too hard work. When this job is over, come over to the Bushnell and I'll get you sent back to Pensacola, get your rate changed to aviation."

Fine. The job was over and by this time, as I say, here was everything all set, we were going to go right into big schools and everything for salvage and diving . . .

Q: And you're going to step out!

Chief Badders: Yes. Well, I went over to the Bushnell to see King and he said, "What do you want?"

I said, "Here's my service number and everything. You were going to send me to Pensacola."

He said, "You're not going to Pensacola. You're going to Washington with Hartley to set up a diving school. You'll do the Navy more good in diving and salvage than you'll ever do as an aviator. Get out of here." That was the end of my aviation.

Q: Were you sorry?

Chief Badders: I was at the time, but later it turned out that I was just as well pleased with the other. I went back aboard ship, and Hartley knew what I had done and I told him what I was going to do, and he said, "You won't get there because I've already arranged for you to go to Washington. I don't know when we'll go, but it won't be long."

And, sure enough, in August of 1928 I went to Washington, and we set up the diving school. By the time I got there the school was pretty well set up.

Q: Where was it located?

Chief Badders: In Washington, at the navy yard. At that time, it was the Washington Gun Factory. When I got there, I went right into the class that was in progress and came out a first class diver. Then Hartley kept me there as an instructor. I stayed there until June of 1930.

Q: How many men would be trained and for how long a period?

Chief Badders: The classes ran six months, and at that time we were using about 20 men in a class--it started with about 20 men and ended up with probably 15 out of the 20.

Q: The others couldn't take it?

Chief Badders: For different reasons they'd flunk out, physically, mostly, and some mentally, and others just didn't have the mechanical ability and things of that kind to cut the mustard.

Q: Then, where were they being employed once they had gone through this course?

Chief Badders: By this time, in addition to the school, they had decided---up until then the Falcon was the only salvage ship they had, but during all this big commotion thing they decided they were going to have more salvage ships, so they took four more of these same type ships and converted them just like the Falcon, put the recompression chambers aboard, the air systems, and all this business, and made billets for personnel aboard in that line of work. We had a submarine rescue vessel with each squadron of submarines. We had one out of New London, Connecticut; we had one out of Panama Canal, Coco Solo Submarine base; we had one at San Diego with the submarines on the West Coast; one in Honolulu; and one in China. Five of them we had, instead of one, and they were all in the areas where the submarines operated. And they built pontoons. They built a complete array of pontoons for each base, and supplied the ships with diving equipment and about everything we had used on the S-51 and S-4 was made available at these points with these different salvage ships.

Badders #1 - 38

Q: This must have automatically given greater assurance to the men who were in submarines.

Chief Badders: I think it did, although we did have problems with submarine men later.

When I went back to the Falcon after the diving school, we used to have submarine drills—this was much later after we'd devised the rescue chamber. A submarine would go out and submerge, then the Falcon or whatever ship the squadron was with—I'm saying the Falcon because I was in her—would go out and locate the submarine, plant a mooring around her, put divers down, hook up a hose to some particular compartment and vent that compartment, and then they'd operate the rescue chambers, take a couple of men out of the submarine with the rescue chamber, and then they would blow up different ballast tanks and raise the submarine. That was the drill.

Before we'd do these drills in New London, we'd know what boat was going out and that would be all we'd know, and I'd take my divers over to the submarine, go over the thing and see what tank we were going to hook up, what ballast tank we were going to hook up to, and what compartment. We kind of rehearsed the thing. I'd try to get the chief of the boat to help me out, cooperate with me, tell me a little about the different parts of the boat, and he'd say, "Oh, the hell with it. Do it yourself. We don't need you. If anything happens to us, we'll take care of ourselves or we'll stay there." So, okay, Buddy, I'll fix you this time.

Well, they went out and they submerged and we found them. When we hooked up the air hose to the compartment, that went all right, but when we hooked up the rescue chamber we opened the hatch and then dumped a bunch of water right down the hatch. We had a lot of trouble hooking up the hose to the deck fitting which required him laying on the bottom three or four hours longer than he would have if he'd been a little more cooperative. We could have brought him up much quicker, but we just wanted to teach him a little lesson!

Q: A hard way to learn!

Chief Badders: But they really had things lined up in pretty good shape after the S-4 job.

Q: Go back to the submarine school again. How deep dives did you make with the students?

Chief Badders: We went to 300 feet on compressed air. I was one of the first ones in the first class to make 300 feet. We started, of course, in shallow water and worked down to that depth. The 300-foot dive was made in the last two or three weeks before the end of the class.

Q: Where would this be, in the Potomac?

Chief Badders: No. These things were simulated, in water, in a tank, with air pressure, simulating the depth.

After leaving the school I went back to the Falcon in 1930, and shortly thereafter I made master diver.

During all this time the S-4 had been patched up and put back in commission--not commission, really, they took the engines and everything out of her, but her hull was tight and she had to be towed everywhere. We took her to Key West and did a lot of experimental work down there with her. Momsen had taken over the perfection of the Momsen lung, as it turned out later.* Also in Key West, we had several prototypes of rescue chambers. We had five or six different types of chambers we worked with, developing a means of bringing the men out in chambers instead of using the Momsen lung.

We spent quite a time down there with that work and we finally ended up selecting this so-called McCann chamber out of the pile.** The Momsen lung was becoming proficient. It had been used in water down to 250 feet and had come to the surface. So the rescue end was pretty well perfected, in Key West off of

---
*Lieutenant Charles B. Momsen, USN, developed the Momsen lung in 1928 and first demonstrated it at the Washington Navy Yard.
**The 10-foot-high McCann chamber was developed by Commander Allen R. McCann, USN, in the late 1930s and used for the first time in an emergency situation to rescue crew members from the USS Squalus (SS-192) in May 1939.

the <u>Falcon</u> with the old <u>S-4</u>. And from that, they built the two lung training tanks, one in New London, Connecticut, and one at Pearl Harbor. All submarine men were trained in the use of the Momsen lung.

Q: At this point, would you describe the Momsen lung?

Chief Badders: A Momsen lung is nothing more than an air bag the men wore on their chests, with a mouthpiece, and they charged the bag with pure oxygen. They could rebreathe that as they came to the surface. To come out of the submarine, they'd have to either flood a compartment or use an escape chamber, come into the chamber with the air pocket in the top, put their mouthpiece in their mouth, and fill their air bag with oxygen similar to filling their spare tire at a gas station, and then they could duck out of this compartment hatch or escape trunk--some submarines had one and some had the other--and slide up a line to the surface, the point being to come to the surface slowly, not come too fast, breathing as they came up. When they got to the surface, they could blow this bag up. If they had used all the oxygen, they could blow it up with their mouth and keep it in place and it acted as a life preserver.

Q: How much time was given them by the lung itself? I mean how much oxygen?

Chief Badders: We used them in water as deep as 300 feet and they had plenty of air because you rebreathe this mixture, and in the lung there was a canister of material that took some of the carbon monoxide out as you rebreathed. The only gas you actually lost out of the bag was through what we called the flutter valve on the bottom of the bag that let the excess air out as you came to the surface, to get that same pressure in that thing all the way to the surface you had at the bottom. Even in 25 or 30 feet of water, the bag would bust before you got to the surface by air expanding.

Q: There's no harm, then, in breathing pure oxygen?

Chief Badders: No, not for a given length of time.

Q: And you say that there were training centers set up in Hawaii and New London for the use of these lungs?

Chief Badders: For training the submarine crews. Every man who qualified for submarine duty had to also be qualified to use the Momsen lung proficiently. Those tanks had 90 feet of water, and they'd come in from the bottom, lock out, and come to the surface. Of course, that was in stages. You'd do it in shallow water and work down. But every man who was in submarines had to be trained in the use of the Momsen lung.

Q: How frequently has that lung been used effectively as a result?

Chief Badders: Actually, to my knowledge, there's never been a real emergency escape with one. And in fact, now they've discontinued it. They don't use it. They found out that a man could come to the surface with nothing just as well as he can with a lung, what we call free escape. Just come up, exhaling as you come, you jump halfway out of the water . . .*

Q: And that's not harmful to the body?

Chief Badders: No, because they're not under pressure.

Q: You mentioned the McCann chamber. Now what is that?

Chief Badders: It's a rescue chamber that was finally perfected to the point where it was the device we used on the Squalus, to rescue all the men off the Squalus later on.

---

*The Momsen lung has been used once in a successful escape attempt from a sunken submarine. On 24 October 1944, the USS Tang (SS-306), commanded by Lieutenant Commander Richard H. O'Kane, USN, the most successful submarine skipper during World War II, was sunk by her own malfunctioning torpedo in Leyte Gulf during her fifth successful war patrol. Of 22 crew members, including O'Kane, who managed to escape the submarine using the Momsen lung, nine survived to be picked up by a Japanese ship and held as prisoners until the end of the war.

The Falcon went back to New London, operating with the submarines, and in May of 1931 I got orders for the Asiatic Fleet. I went to Tsingtao, China.

Q: Was this something you sought? Did you want to go out there?

Chief Badders: No, nobody wanted to go to the Asiatic Fleet, particularly a married man, a family man, like me. I had two children at that time, a son and a daughter, and I didn't want to go to China Station, but somebody had to go. They only had one master diver out there. They were supposed to have four, and the one they had, his tour of duty was way overdue and he had left, so actually when I got out there there wasn't any, except me.

Anyway, I got ordered to China. I went aboard the Pigeon in Tsingtao.

Q: And your family had to stay here?

Chief Badders: I didn't take my family out there, because the Pigeon and the submarines would operate five months out of Manila, and then we'd take a month to go to China and operate five months in China, then make the same trip back. We were operating all the time. We were out practically every day, except some weekends we'd get in. Once in a while, we'd have a week or two lay-in at Mariveles or Manila, and sometimes in China we'd lay in a week in Tsingtao or somewhere in that area.

Well, I was the only master diver on the whole Asiatic Station. I had ten first class divers on the Pigeon, 12 second class, and I had anywhere from eight to ten first class divers on the Canopus. We had to keep those men requalified. Regulations required a man to make four dives every six-month period to retain his qualification, which meant we had some diving to do. In each case we'd get some projects on the bottom to try to keep the men in some kind of training for any disaster that might come along. Fortunately, we had no submarine disasters during my time out there.

Q: Incidentally, was it similar for the submarine, requiring to dive frequently, and the men got extra pay as a result? Did divers get anything?

Chief Badders: Yes, a first class diver got $15 a month. A master diver got $20, a second class diver got $10, and if you made a dive more than 150 feet you got 20 cents a foot for one dive. You could only earn a certain amount of money. If you made ten dives, you only got paid for one. You could make as much as $30 a month extra pay, but this would only happen about once every six months. But, as I say, a master diver got $20 a month; that was as long as you were qualified.

Q: Was there any difference in diving in the Far East, as contrasted with the Atlantic?

Chief Badders: No, there was practically no difference. There was some difference in the undersea light. For instance, in Mariveles Bay we were making some night dives and using a diving light. The custom was for the master diver to make the first dive. Then he can come up and be on deck to take charge of all the other diving operations as diving officer.

Q: He surveys the situation?

Chief Badders: Right, supposedly. So I made the first dive; I hit the bottom. I wasn't down there very long when I see all these, I thought, little eels about the size of my thumb in diameter and about a foot long and they were darting around this light. Some of them got inside the wire mesh protecting the bulb of the light, and I told them topside to take the light up, it was only creating a disturbance down there, eels and things were attracted by the light so that it was doing more harm than good. So they pulled the light up on deck, and I heard a commotion over the telephone up there, and I couldn't imagine what it was. Then I got orders to come up. I came on up waiting for decompression. It took me about half an hour to get out of the water. I'd been diving in about 160 feet of water, and when I got up, a pharmacist's mate while I was on the decompression station said, "Look at your hands. Make sure your hands are not scratched up." Your hands are the only thing not protected in the water, you know. I couldn't see any scratches or anything on my hands, and that's all he said.

Then I found out that these damned things weren't eels; they were coral snakes. I must have landed right in a bed of them because there were millions of them down there.

Q: They're poisonous!

Chief Badders: Very poisonous. They're little black snakes, they never get very big. Panamanian fishermen brought them up by the bundle sometimes in their fish nets, and they'd pick them up by the tail and knock their heads off on the side of the boat.

Q: They're more deadly than rattlesnakes!

Chief Badders: That's right. At that time, out there, they'd say if you were bitten by a coral snake, that's it, you've had it. I guess maybe I was lucky, I didn't get the least scratch or anything, but they were more interested in the light than they were in me. They probably didn't even see me; the light would blind them.

While I was out there we got an SOS—we were in the China Sea at the time—and we went to see what it was all about. It was a ship on fire, apparently a Japanese ship, the Kaku Maru. The crew had all abandoned her already and was all out in lifeboats, and we went alongside and started pumping water into her. We fought the fire for 24 hours and put it out. The crew came aboard and by this time the engine room was all out of commission; the fire had burned, and the cargo had never caught fire. We had looked in the cargo hatches and the hatches were all coal from what we could see, so we figured it was a cargo of coal going to Japan.

Later this ship was brought in to Manila Bay and they started to unload this thing, take the coal out of her, and there were only 3 or 4 or 5 feet of coal on top of five-gallon cans of aviation gasoline in cases, two cans in a case. Every one of the cargo holds was full of cans of aviation gasoline. If the fire had ever gotten to the cargo holds, we'd have been blown sky-high, everybody.

Q: What was the purpose of disguising it?

Chief Badders: I don't know, never did find out just why they did that. There had to be some reason, trying to smuggle the stuff in or tax or duty or something. I don't know.

Q: That's why they abandoned ship so quickly!

Chief Badders: Yes, absolutely. They thought the fire was going to get into that gasoline. They weren't going to stay there and try to fight it. They got off. They could have probably put it out if they'd stayed aboard and kept their firerooms going for steam for pumps. They could have pumped water, but they just pulled fires and beat it! And they didn't tell us anything until way the next night, and our crew was really hostile with those people. We finally brought them aboard the Pigeon and fed them and let them wash up and things of that kind, and they still didn't say anything. Some other commercial company brought it in, unloaded her, and they called our skipper over.

Q: That was an example of their secrecy.

Chief Badders: Yes. There was another passenger ship that hit the rocks and turned over on her side, and we did some work on that. We didn't salvage it. The Japanese themselves went in and salvaged that. On this fire thing, I got a letter of commendation from the Commander in Chief of the Asiatic Fleet.

Q: What was that at the time?

Chief Badders: It wasn't Hart. It was the man ahead of Hart.*

---

*Admiral Thomas C. Hart, USN, Commander Asiatic Fleet from 1939 to 1942.

Q: Yarnell?*

Chief Badders: Might have been. It was a funny thing about that passenger ship. She hit the beach and hit the rocks and she was rolling over on her side as she flooded, and never would have been completely under water, of course, because she was aground, but the passengers were abandoning this thing. They'd come down the high side of that ship on lines and hang onto those things with their feet out of the water. They threw hundreds of lines over the side, and these people would hang on the lines with their feet and knees pulled up under their chest, wouldn't even get their feet in the water, until they'd almost pass out and then they'd drop off the lines and damned if a lot of them didn't drown. If they'd had sense enough to let themselves into the water and take their weight off themselves, we could have rescued dozens more than we did. Twenty-five or 30 people died before we could get to them. They couldn't understand what we were trying to tell them, to get in the water and hold onto the line. There were lifeboats out there trying to pick the people up and instead of picking up people they were picking up suitcases. People had thrown suitcases and great big old grass bags overboard, and the people were picking them up instead of picking up the people. The Japanese took that over and salvaged her and brought her in.

---

*Admiral Harry E. Yarnell, USN, Commander Asiatic Fleet from 1936 to 1939.

Q: Did the British have any salvage operations out there?

Chief Badders: They had some with their submarine squadron out of Hong Kong, nothing near to what we had on the Pigeon, though. Just how much they did have I don't know, but I do know that they weren't nearly as well equipped as we were. For instance, they didn't have a salvage vessel designated as such, and the only divers they had were on the tender.

Q: In Far Eastern waters, were sharks a problem?

Chief Badders: Not a problem, really. We had them. Also in Mariveles Bay I guess there's more sharks per square foot there than any place else in the world that I've ever been, but they didn't bother anybody. They were nosy. They'd swim up close to you and look around, but you make a quick move and they're gone. If you ever got excited and maybe cut one of them and started blood flowing around, that might have been a different story, they'd start fighting among themselves. But we never had anyone from the boats be attacked by a shark.

That was something in Key West when we were working on the Momsen lung, which meant that we were just in swimming trunks coming out of a tank we had on the bottom and coming to the surface. Around Key West and Dry Tortugas and all that area down there is alive with barracuda, and those things were flocking around in our area pretty rapidly. We finally became so concerned about them that we built a big square of netting and put this tank down inside it so that the barracuda couldn't get through. They were notorious for getting things that were shiny and bright, and we had a lot of valves and things on these lungs and we were afraid they might snap at them and grab a hand or something.

Badders #2 - 53

Interview Number 2 with Chief Machinist's Mate William Badders
U.S. Navy (Retired)

Place: Chief Badders's home in Annapolis, Maryland

Date: Wednesday morning, 22 September 1971

Subject: Biography

Interviewer: John T. Mason, Jr.

Q: It's very good to see you again this morning, sir. Now I hope you'll resume your account of your tour of duty with the Asiatic Fleet.

Chief Badders: I don't remember just exactly where we were when we cut off the last time you were here, but I believe it was diving operations in Mariveles Bay.

Q: That is it precisely.

Chief Badders: That was just one of the many experiences we had out there. The diving conditions were not the best normally. Fortunately, most diving that we did, we had no real accidents, particularly in our Navy. We had some work to do for other shipping outfits that didn't pertain to diving. There were two cases of fire, one a grounding and the _Pigeon_ was involved more in saving the vessel. The grounding was trying to save some of the people that were abandoning their ship. It was a Japanese passenger liner that had run aground and was turning over on the rocks as she flooded, and the passengers were slipping down the side on lines and whatnot and going into the water. The crew had lifeboats in the water, but they appeared to be more interested in picking up luggage and stuff of that kind that had been thrown overboard than they were the passengers. The consequences were that some of the people died. We never did know how many, but we did know that some few drowned.

Q: Life is considered somewhat cheaper out in the Far East!

Chief Badders: Yes. Evidently the crew just hadn't been trained in rescue, for one thing. At least, they didn't appear to be. They didn't appear to know how to handle their boats, to maneuver them around among the debris and people. It was just a very disorganized-looking operation. The captain of the Pigeon worked the Pigeon right alongside the vessel, and we took all the people aboard that we could handle. Then we lay off of the wreck for a while; then were told to get out of there, that the Japanese Government would take over, which they did. We turned the passengers over to some other ship that came alongside and we left. Some months later, we were in Tsingtao, China, with the submarine division, and they brought the ship in. They had refloated her and were noticed as she went by where we were anchored they had cofferdamed the whole length of the vessel, pumped her out, and brought her in more or less laying on her side. I understood at that time that they rebuilt the ship and recommissioned her and she went back into service.

We had one other experience. We had an SOS, got to the area, and found a ship burning. The crew had abandoned the ship and were in boats, laying off. We went right alongside and started pumping water aboard and fighting the fire. We fought the fire for about 30 hours and finally extinguished it altogether. It was mostly staterooms and things of that kind that were burning, mostly topside fires. It never did get down in the cargo holds. We had looked at the cargo and assumed that it was coal. Everything that we could see in the hatches was coal, pulverized coal, so we had no concern really of danger as far as the fire was concerned of explosions and things of that kind. This was a Japanese ship, Japanese crew, Japanese flag.

They had in the meantime brought these men who were in the lifeboats aboard the Pigeon and fed them. They couldn't speak to them very well. Very few of them could speak any English and we didn't have any people aboard who could speak much Japanese, so we didn't get many details. But they wouldn't go near the ship until the fire was completely out. We wondered why they had abandoned because it didn't appear to be too awfully bad, except it was a contrary fire to put out.

Some time later we were in Manila and we saw this same ship come in under tow and being unloaded in Manila Bay. We paid very little attention to it, except we happened to look over one day and we see small wooden cases leaving the ship in cargo nets. We wondered what they were. We hadn't seen anything like that in the holds we'd inspected. Then we went over to see what was going on. A couple of us were curious, so we got the boat and went alongside. The contractor that had salvaged this thing and brought it in had discovered that these cargo holds, particularly the forward holds—I'm not sure they were all that way—were full of five-gallon cans, two cans in a case, and these cans contained high-test aviation gasoline. Evidently they were smuggling this stuff into Japan or wherever they were going—we assumed they were on their way to Japan—and they had put these cases in the lower part of the hold and put about a 10-foot layer of pulverized coal over the top of them. We couldn't imagine any other reason for it being there except to fool somebody about the type of cargo they had.

Then, of course, it became clear to us why the Japanese crew had left the vessel. They were afraid the fire was going to get into that gasoline. If it ever had, it'd have been a real explosion.

That was about the extent of my experience of salvage out there. As I say, fortunately, we had no submarine accidents of any kind. Oh, we had the usual once or twice—mooring lines and propellers and things of that kind which were more or less routine.

The rest of our diving was just more or less a continuation of training, re-qualifying our divers. At that time, and I assume it's still in effect, first class divers, master divers, and second class divers had to make four dives every six months in given depths of water to retain their qualification. So that required about four days out of every six months for diving operations. Sometimes we got four days in succession; sometimes they'd be split up, one day a month or something like that. The first class and master divers had to make their dives in 150 feet of water or more, and the second class were required to go 90 feet and perform some task on the bottom. We used to cook up different things for the divers to do on the bottom.

Then we had scheduled what we termed search, rescue, and blow operations. A submarine would go out and submerge on the bottom. The *Pigeon* would go out and locate it, tie a mooring round it, and we would send divers down to hook up salvage hoses to the compartments and circulate air through a compartment, blow a ballast tank, operate the rescue chamber through either the fore or the after hatch, take a couple of men out of the submarine. This was to keep the equipment in operating condition and the crew trained in the type of work that we would have to do if we did have an accident or anything.

Q: May I ask, what is the maximum depth for comfortable diving?

Chief Badders: At that time our first class divers and master divers—they could be qualified first class or master if they were capable of going to only 150 feet, but we preferred to have them qualified to a depth of 300 feet, and most of us were.

Q: What's the difference in technique required?

Chief Badders: The pressure effect on the men's systems was what governed how deep they could go. Some men could take more pressure than others and retain their senses of direction and capability of performing tasks. Pressure affects different people in different ways. I'm speaking strictly of using compressed air as a breathing medium, because we hadn't got into the helium-oxygen gases yet.

We tried to make our re-qualifying dives for first class and master divers between 150 and 200 feet, somewhere in that neighborhood. Very rarely did we put men down over 200 feet because it took extra time for decompression and it wasn't likely—well, you're just as likely to have an accident in 200 feet of water as in 100 feet, but it was figured 200 feet would be about the normal working depth for first class divers. We tried to keep our men well-trained and in physical condition to go 150 to 200 feet at any time they'd be called on to go down and do any kind of a task that they were qualified to do.

That just about took care of all the diving operations.

At that time the Pigeon had dual duty. Her primary function, of course, was working with the submarines on the surface, towing targets, and maneuvering with them, and things of that kind, which required the majority of our time. Although diving and salvage were primary requirements for her out there--and that applied to all the rest of the salvage ships we had in the Navy at that time---they all had other things to do that appeared to be more important than the diving and the salvage program they were supposed to carry out.

Q: Well, diving and salvage are related to emergencies, aren't they?

Chief Badders: Yes, and of course the farther apart the emergencies come up, the less interest is shown toward that type of work. You'd say, "Well, we haven't had an accident in three or four years. It looks like we're not going to have any for a while so we have other things that are more important to do."

We had other activities out there. I played a lot of golf in Manila, and some in China, not too much. I played baseball in a professional league in Manila. In China I played with the submarine division team and my team coach and manager at that time was a submarine captain, Lieutenant Roscoe Good. He later became a vice admiral and had one of the big commands in the Far

East.*

We won the championship, too, by the way, three years in a row under his coaching and management. When he was sent to the Far East, I sent him a letter and told him that it was quite a jump from lieutenant and baseball manager to go up to supreme command. I had a nice reply from him that he still remembered the old days and the baseball and what wonderful duty it was.

Q: Athletics must have been a very important element for the crew on duty so far away from home.

Chief Badders: Well, it was a source of entertainment. There wasn't much for people to do out there except go sightseeing. If they didn't want to hang around the gin mills and dance halls and places drinking and hanging round with the girls, there wasn't much to do except go to baseball games or any other entertainment that the Navy could cook up. So this baseball was a great thing. We played as often as we could and practiced a lot which, in turn, turned out some pretty good teams. We had the submarine division team and the destroyer division team, and the heavy cruisers had a team. Then the individual ships had teams. Individual destroyers had teams, and they played against each other. It created quite a bit of entertainment for people that

---
*Lieutenant Roscoe F. Good, USN, who later held the three-star billet of Commander Naval Forces Far East from 1956 to 1957.

were interested in athletics.

A great number of the enlisted men played golf, particularly in Manila, at the old municipal golf course. We used to run tournaments and things out there among ourselves and we had quite a time. By the way, I made a hole in one on the municipal golf course in 1933, on April fifth, which is my son's birthday, so I thought that was quite an occasion. It just proves that a hole in one has to be all luck. It can't be science, because I was probably the worst golfer that ever golfed, but somehow or other on a par-three hole I got lucky enough to roll the ball in on my drive.

I have gone ashore on Sunday morning and played 18 holes of golf and sometimes another nine. We would play 18, then go to the 19th in the old Manila Hotel, have a sandwich and a stein of beer, and if we felt real good we'd go out and play another nine. Then I'd get out of my golf shorts into baseball uniform right in the locker room and head for the baseball park and play a baseball doubleheader in the afternoon. As I said, the league in Manila was a professional league. It had two military teams from different Army positions around there. They had a team from the Cavite Navy Yard, a civilian team from in town sponsored by one of the rubber companies, either Goodyear or Goodrich. Then the only place in the world that I ever heard of a college playing professional baseball, the University of the Philippines team played in the league.

It was strictly a professional league, because you signed contracts and you got a salary, just like the leagues here in the States. It was a good league. It compared to, oh, I'd say AA ball in the States.* We not only played among ourselves, the league schedule, but we played independent teams that would come down from Japan. I played against the American League All-Stars. Lou Gehrig brought a team out one year.** Then I played against the colored team that Satchel Paige brought out there, two years.*** I hit the longest ball I ever hit in my life off of Satchel Paige. Strictly luck again, the same as my hole in one in golf. He had a three-and-two count on me, and I knew what the next pitch was going to be. It was one of his high, hard ones that he could throw and make it look like a golf ball coming at you. Well, I started swinging when he started winding up and I caught the ball just right and knocked it completely out of the park. The hardest ball I ever hit.

We'd gather an all-star team from our league and play them, and then we'd take an all-star team from the military organizations and play them. They ended up playing five or six

---

*At the time, AA was the top classification in minor league professional baseball.
**Henry Louis Gehrig (1903-1941), longtime first baseman for the New York Yankees, most valuable player in the American League in 1936.
***Leroy "Satchel" Paige (1906-1982), star pitcher in the Negro League from 1924 to 1948, entered the major leagues at the age of 42 and played five years with the Cleveland Indians and the St. Louis Browns.

games in Manila, and then they'd go on to Japan and different places. I enjoyed playing with those colored people more than any baseball I ever played, I believe, because you could certainly learn things from them. They were, without a doubt, the finest baseball players in the game at the time.

Paige would pitch not every day but every other day anyway, because, after all, he was the big drawing card. The thing about Paige, at that time he not only was an outstanding pitcher, but he could hit a ball anywhere any time he wanted to. We had some darned good pitchers out in that league. We had a couple of Marines out there who quit the service and came up and played in the Texas League. Another man who was pitching for us quit the Navy and came up and pitched in the International League. So they had to be pretty good ballplayers. I've seen Paige stand in the batter's box until he got two strikes on him and he'd point to one of the outfielders to put him in position and tell him that's where he was going to hit the next pitch that got over the plate. And, sure enough, he hit a line drive or a ball almost in the man's hands out there, if he didn't want to get a hit. If he wanted a hit, of course, he'd try to put it somewhere else. If he needed a run or two or he didn't need a run, it was just showmanship, he'd just drive the ball to a particular man in the outfield against one of these pretty good pitchers.

We had a lot of fun with the colored fellows. We never beat them. We couldn't beat them. We'd come close, and they'd turn on the works and go just as far as they had to go to keep from losing.

That's about all the athletics we had out there. We didn't play basketball, but we had fighters. We had fighters and wrestlers in the fleet, and they were pretty active. I never did go in for any of that. I guess I was a little old for it. I wasn't cut out for fighting and wrestling, anyway.

Q: What percentage of the men would you say went in for athletics of one kind of another?

Chief Badders: Percentagewise, it's kind of hard to say. On my particular ship there was only myself and one other man that played baseball. Our crew was too small to have a team in the ship. The two of us played with the submarine division team. So that was two out of, say, 75. That's a darned small percentage.

Q: Yes, it is.

Chief Badders: We didn't have any fighters or wrestlers. We had 10 or 12--I'm speaking strictly of the enlisted men now--that played golf. I think just about all the officers played golf. I would say maybe 10% of the crew of the majority of the bigger ships would be in some type of fleet competition--what you'd call in school intramural stuff. They had boat crews, some boat racing, whaleboat racing and stuff of that kind. There was no track, basketball, or any of that kind of thing. I didn't even see swimming events. It seemed to me that would have been a good sport to produce out there, but I didn't ever see any of that going on. Primarily baseball and fighting and wrestling in the fleet just about took care of all the competitive athletics. Playing golf, of course, didn't amount to much.

So in 1934 I was playing ball. We were getting ready for a fleet championship, and Lieutenant Good had our team up in Olongapo getting some practice for the first championship game we were going to play the coming weekend. I used to slide when I was going into a base on a close play. I'd slide on my chest and go in headfirst and only give the baseman a hand to tag at when I went into the bag. I was trying to score on an infield ball and I made my dive for the plate. I went too far, my spikes kind of carried too far, and I rolled over. I stuck my arm out to protect myself, and my elbow stuck in the sand and shoved my arm all the way up to my neck, tore my shoulder all to pieces. I went to the hospital. They fortunately had a great bone surgeon in the Cañacao hospital at that time, in Cavite, and he fixed my arm up real well. It took about three months to do it.

In the meantime my enlistment had expired—my enlistment expired before that, but they were keeping me out there overtime because they hadn't sent another master diver out there to relieve me. I think the commanding officer of the _Pigeon_ thought that I hurt my arm intentionally to get off of the ship so I could catch a transport to come home. The prime thought in everybody's mind out there was what transport you were going to get to get home.

I remember one time I was back on the fantail of the <u>Pigeon</u> sitting on a winch. I'd been fishing and I had my fishline off of the reel going down into a manhole going into what we called the after cargo hold of the ship. I'd been drying the line off, and I was reeling it back up. The captain walked back to the fantail and he saw me there with this fish pole and reel with the line down a manhole going into the after hold. He said, "What are you fishing for in there?"

I said, "I'm fishing for a transport. I'm trying to get out of here. See if I can't catch a transport."

He said, "Well, give me that rod and move over. I'm looking for one, too."

But, of course, that's not the reason I tore my arm up. I ended up doing a little over three months in the hospital and, as I said, by that time I was about four months overtime on my enlistment. They loaded me on a transport and sent me back to the States. I was discharged in San Francisco and reenlisted right away. I came here to Washington and looked around to see what kind of a billet I could get. There was nothing open at the diving school, experimental unit for a master diver. I had never had duty on the West Coast, and there was a billet open in the old USS Holland, submarine tender and repair ship, for a master diver. So I asked them to send me out there and they did.

The family and I went out. We drove across country. First time I ever drove a car across the country. I bought a big old Buick and passed everything on the road but a gas station. I went broke before I got to California and had to send a telegram to friends of mine to meet me with some money in Phoenix, Arizona. I didn't have enough money to make the rest of the trip. I had enough to get to Phoenix, and when I got there I'd be broke. Sure enough, when I got there I had some money waiting for me at the telegraph office, to get the rest of the way out to San Diego.

I had a very pleasant tour of duty on the Holland. There, athletics was a big thing. I had a nice bunch of equipment on the Holland, diving equipment, and she was designed to make a lift over her bow. She had big sheaves up in her bow that could be rigged for making a lift, I think capable of about 80 or 90 tons. We never used it during my time on the ship but it was there in case we ever needed it. I think it was there primarily to assist in changing propellers, to lift the stern out of the water for propeller changes. I never saw it used all the time I was on the ship.

There, again, diving was a very primary activity. They had also in San Diego the Ortolan, a salvage and rescue vessel the same as the Falcon and the Pigeon, and when it came time for me and my divers on the Holland to make our re-qualifying dives we were sent to the Ortolan for three or four days and we'd go out in deep water and make our dives. That's about all the diving we did in the Holland, re-qualifying dives. I used to take my second class divers out in a motorboat and put them down in 90 feet of water from a motor launch, using high-pressure air for them to breathe.

I was active again in baseball and football. I wasn't able to play much baseball at that time. My arm never did completely recover from the accident I had in the Philippines. We had a real good baseball team on the ship. We played different ships around that area and civilian teams ashore. By the way, my team---I was manager and coach of the team on the Holland---played the San Diego high school some practice games and Ted Williams was playing ball for the San Diego high school at that time.* Even then, and this was in 1936, we could never get him out. He'd just drive the ball down somebody's throat in the infield or send it out of the park. He was quite a ballplayer even when he was a high school boy. Of course, none of us ever thought at that time he'd ever become the great ballplayer that he did.

That was strictly a ship's team, and then we had the submarine division football team that operated from the Holland.

---
*Theodore S. Williams (1918-   ), longtime (1938-1960) outfielder for the Boston Red Sox, was the most valuable player in the American League in 1946, earned six batting titles during his career, and is a member of baseball's Hall of Fame.

All the equipment and everything was on the Holland, and the players came from the Holland and all the submarines. We had a real good football team. Oscar Hagberg was the regular coach.* He was executive on one of the submarines at the time. He later became head coach here at the Academy. I don't remember the years he was head coach here, but he had a very successful time. I guess he might have been one of the last active duty coaches that the Academy had.** I'm not sure about that either because while all this was going on I was in the Panama Canal. But I was one of his assistant coaches for the football team. We used to leave the ship every day at noon during the football season, go to the foot of Broadway, where the Navy had an athletic field. We kept all our equipment in a locker room ashore, and we'd practice all afternoon about four days a week, and we played our games on Saturdays, sometimes on a Sunday, but generally our games were on Saturday afternoons. We played everybody. We played the different ships, the battleships up in San Pedro, and the different division teams around. We played San Diego State College, scrimmaged against them about twice a week, every week. We won way more games than we lost. Our big competitor there was the Marine Base. The San Diego Marine Base had a crackerjack

---

*Lieutenant (junior grade) Oscar E. Hagberg, USN, then serving in the USS Bonita (SS-165).
**As a lieutenant commander in 1944-1945, Hagberg compiled a 13-4-1 record as head coach of the Naval Academy football team. He was succeeded by another active duty naval officer, Captain Thomas J. Hamilton, USN.

team, too, but they didn't play quite the way we did. For some reason, they didn't seem to have quite the same rules. We could only have two officers on our team, whether they were playing or not. There could only be two men who were considered players on the team. That was the Navy regulation.

Q: What would be the reason for that?

Chief Badders: Well, you could pad a team up with Naval Academy graduates, stars from the Naval Academy, and have a much better team than the one that didn't have the number of officers aboard. And, after all, they figured that this type of endeavor was an enlisted man's activity anyway, not so much for the officers. But the Marines had a regulation that they could play two men at a time. They could have as many officers on their team as they wanted so long as they didn't have more than two playing at a time. I don't know why their regulations didn't come under the same heading as ours because I always figured a Marine was a sailor with his---well, I won't say what I was going to say---but they should have come under the same regulations we did. Anyhow, they would have some pretty good ex-college men, a couple of Naval Academy men and they played pretty good football. They used to give us about as much trouble as anybody we played. Always good clean rivalry and a lot of fun.

Well, in 1936 one of my old commanding officers from the

Pigeon had taken over the experimental diving unit in Washington, and I received a letter from the Navy Department--we were on a maneuver to the Panama Canal. When we arrived in Panama and the mail came on board, I had this letter from the Navy Department, from the man who detailed divers all over the Navy, telling me that Lieutenant Commander Hollowell had requested that I be considered for duty at the experimental diving unit.* At that time, that was strictly volunteer duty and I didn't have to accept it if I didn't want it.

So I wrote right back and told them I would accept it, because I was very interested in what was going on and what was expected to go on in the experimental diving unit. When the fleet got back to San Diego, I was detached and transferred to Washington.

Q: That intrigues me. What was expected to be developed at the diving unit?

Chief Badders: Right at that time, I wasn't sure of everything that was going on, but I knew that underwater burning and welding were being developed. I had been with underwater burning in the Navy from the time we used it on the S-51, and I'd had about as much experience with it as anybody in the Navy at that time. I

---
*Lieutenant Commander John A. Hollowell, Jr., USN.

thought that I could be some help to them there in developing the technique and equipment. So anyhow, I accepted the duty at the experimental unit, and when the fleet returned to San Diego, I was transferred to Washington.

For the first year or so we devoted most of our time to underwater burning, both gas and electric arc, and underwater welding. It just started at that time, 1936. We had many crude tools to work with, in the welding particularly, and we spent our time redeveloping these things and getting material and equipment that we could really work with. It became apparent in a short time that arc welding could be done underwater.

Q: This would be on the exterior, on the hull?

Chief Badders: Yes.

Q: Would you explain that a little more, the method?

Chief Badders: Well, it's done exactly the same way it is on the surface except that the electrode holder must be insulated from salt water, or any water, fresh or salt, and the electrode that was being used must have an insulated coating on it to protect it from the water. Otherwise, the arc would go out the side of the rod, which has happened many times, and we had a bubble in the insulating material. We used many different insulating materials, trying different things out. We started out with beeswax, dipping the rods in molten beeswax. Then we used cellophane dissolved in acetone, dipped the rods in that, and that was a pretty good insulating material. Later there was some commercial stuff that was used to dip these electrodes in. You use the same electrodes that you use on the surface welding, except in this instance it was dipped in this insulating material before it was used underwater. The method of welding was almost exactly the same as welding on the surface.

Q: At what depth was it feasible?

Chief Badders: Any depth. Depth has very little effect on welding. Originally the idea was that you just wouldn't be able to strike an arc in water. It had to be an area where there wasn't any water. We used different things to try to make little air pockets for the electrode to work in, similar to the gas-burning torch, but, of course, that didn't work. Then we found that the arc would form itself underwater just as it would on the surface, almost the same. The arc is so hot that it created its own air pocket around itself. The thing about underwater welding, of course, is that it's cooled much quicker than it is on the surface and it becomes brittle. But I had welders in the Panama Canal—we'll get to that later but it's a good time to mention it here.

We developed welding in the Panama Canal to the point where I could take expert welders out of a boiler shop or a shipfitter's shop and make divers out of them, and they could perform welds underwater on ship hulls and things of that nature with 80% of the efficiency that they would get in the boiler shop. So that would be darned good temporary repair and, in some cases, they proved permanent.

Q: In some cases it didn't have to be done over again?

Chief Badders: Right. Then the Bureau of Mines Safety Appliance Corporation in Pittsburgh came out with a new tool. At that time, they called it the velocity power tool that drove steel projectiles into steel plates for bolting up plates over holes and hollows and things of that kind. That was a lot of work perfecting that unit. They had four or five different tools. They had one for driving in studs, one gun would drive a solid stud in a plate with a threaded end on it, put a nut on it, slip a plate over the stud, and hold another plate down. The same gun fired a hollow stud that you could drive through the hull of a boat and hook something up to it, an air hose, and circulate air through it---a small stud, of course, but after all it would be enough air to sustain life in a compartment, which we could have done, for instance, going way back on the S-4 job if we'd had something of that nature. We could have slammed it in the hull of the S-4 in that forward torpedo room and circulated some fresh air and kept those men alive.

Then they had a so-called rivet expander. It would drive a stud into the center of a loose rivet and expand it, tighten it up. A cable cutter for cutting steel cable up to about an inch and a half in diameter. These things were all fired like firing a gun. The projectiles had a firing cap and were loaded with powder, and that's the secret of the whole tool. The number of grains of powder in the load determined how thick a plate you could drive a given stud into. We had studs that were good for from 3/8 plate up to 1-1/8 inch, but, of course, the thicker the plate, the more powder had to be in. These studs were all marked with the plate thickness that they were designed for.

That required a lot of time, bringing these tools to the point where they could be used. They were developed, or at least they were accepted primarily by the Navy, for fire control work aboard ship, and they could be used in many phases of salvage. I used it extensively in the Panama Canal later.

We were diving deeper in the unit by that time. Most of the men there—I guess all of them—were qualified for 300 feet when they left the diving school. We had another master diver there and myself, two masters, and ten first class divers. We were considered to be guinea pigs more than anything else when it came to diving, for working out new decompression tables to prevent the bends and other tables for treating the bends for the men who were afflicted with them.

Helium and oxygen mixtures were just beginning to see the light of day as a breathing medium for deeper diving. There had been some experiments with this gas as a breathing medium back in 1925. Gunner Tibbals and two or three men had done a little bit of work with it, but it never was developed to any extent.* But it was known that it could be used as a breathing medium, and it had two advantages over compressed air--one that the men could dive deeper. When you go as far as 300 feet with compressed air, it affects the thinking ability of the men. You get two or three different symptoms. One, you're over-exhilarated; you think you can do great things and think you are doing great things when you're doing nothing except getting in trouble. Another condition is the man just more or less passes out. Oxygen exhilaration is what it amounts to, because, at that pressure, the oxygen content of the air is just too great for men to breathe. So the oxygen content has to be cut down to go any deeper, and that's exactly what the helium would do. Instead of mixing helium with compressed air, they'd mix oxygen with helium and bring the oxygen content to the percentage required for the depth the man was going.

We were working with this and getting some results, not too good, but we had designed a re-breathing system for the diving helmet where the gas could be recirculated through the helmet and

---
*Chief Gunner Clarence L. Tibbals, USN.

breathed over, because you couldn't just shoot helium and oxygen through an exhaust valve to the surface like you did compressed air. It was too expensive and too big a problem of supplying it.

Q: Was there any special danger, too, in handling helium?

Chief Badders: No. Helium is a very safe gas to have. In fact, I would rather have helium—our helium was all handled in steel flasks like the oxygen, and I'd rather handle the helium bottles than the oxygen bottles. There was always the possibility of fire over the oxygen and, of course, helium was just nothing. We never had any problem at any time with either one of them really, but I think oxygen would create more of a hazard at any time than helium would in storage and handling. Of course, anything under that high pressure—those bottles are charged up to 1,000 pounds—there's always the potential for an explosion of some kind, something tearing away.

We went ahead with our deeper diving with the helium, and we'd go down to about 350 feet, I guess. We had worked out recompression tables, both for diving and for treatment of bends, in the tanks of the experimental unit, and then we went to the Falcon in New London and went out and did the same things in the open sea. That was a cold-water operation. They wanted to prove these both in cold water and in warm water. So we went to the Falcon out of New London and went up around Portsmouth and the

Boston area, up in through there, and tried these tables in cold water to see if it made any difference to the effect on the human body.

Later we went to the Mallard in the Panama Canal to do the same thing. Working these tables, we'd start at 100 feet. We'd put all the divers down, like today we'd be down 100 feet and run the tables that were designed for that depth. Then the next day we'd go out to 125 feet, and 200 feet and on down. Well, we had worked up to the 200-foot depth and each time we made a new depth it had generally become my function to make the first dive at each new depth. We were making a 225-foot dive way out in the Pacific from the Panama Canal--when I say way out I mean 100 miles or so out, somewhere between the Panama Canal and Cocos Island--and I got dressed to go down. We'd been diving in the tropical waters there which are warm, of course, and I was using under my diving dress a pair of dungaree trousers and sweatshirt, well, undershorts, of course, and that was all the clothes I had on. We used our diving dress with the cuff on it and not the gloves, which meant your hands were exposed.

I started down, and I got almost to the bottom on this descending line and something hit me just like ice skating and the ice had broken and I'd fallen in the water. It was just that cold, that quick. I told topside, over the phone, to stop me, there was something wrong, hold me there for a minute. Meantime I stopped myself as best I could from sliding down this line. I said, "I'm freezing down here. It's cold. I'm about to freeze." Nobody would believe me, so I said, "Well, my hands are getting numb, it's so cold, I can't control my valves. You'd better take me up out of here and find out what this is."

Well, they were still debating up there. They thought old Bill Badders had finally gone nuts or something. So I said, "If you don't bring me up, I'm going to blow up," and I began to lighten up my suit and up I went. I was only down for a minute or two, so it required practically no decompression. I think I stopped at 10 feet for a few minutes and then came on up.

Commander Hollowell wanted to know what had happened to me, and I said, "I don't know what it was, but there's something down there. Just all of a sudden you hit cold water. It's actually so cold that you've got to be prepared for it. You've got to have the dress with gloves on it and wear heavy underwear, or you're going to be too cold to dive."

So they put a maximum and minimum thermometer down and, sure enough, the temperature of the water changed from 70-some degrees to down in the 40s. It was that Humboldt Current coming in there, underwater. They didn't realize it was in that area. So we had to move operations. We weren't getting any warm-water dive there, at that depth. We had to move out of that particular area and get warm-water diving.

We finished that operation in the Canal Zone and went on back to Washington. About that time Hollowell was detached, and

Momsen took command of the experimental diving—Swede Momsen who, previous to that, had developed the Momsen lung.* Then we really got going on the helium and oxygen procedure of diving, and we were working down deeper and deeper all the time. I don't just remember the year, but it must have been 1937 when McDonald, the other master diver in the unit, and myself, made a dive apiece at 500 feet in the simulated dives in water under pressure in the diving tank, using helium and oxygen, and we came out with no ill effects.** And the beautiful thing about these dives, as I said, with compressed air anything over 100 feet you would have been very inefficient. You'd have not been able to think clearly and do things that you should be able to do on the bottom. But with helium and oxygen you were practically normal, almost as normal as on the surface, and we proved that by doing mathematical problems and conversation and other things. So these 500-feet dives were made with no effects at all. Neither one of us had the bends. Our recompression table proved efficient.

Then again we left the unit and went to the Falcon in New London. We were going to make these same dives in the open sea. Here again we were working down a few feet each day. We had just got to 375 feet, I guess, and we had bad weather—fog, as no

---

*Lieutenant Commander Charles B. Momsen, USN.
**Chief Metalsmith James H. McDonald, USN, who later was awarded a Medal of Honor for his part in the May 1939 rescue of the crew of the USS Squalus (SS-192).

place else in the world has it like Portsmouth, New Hampshire. We just couldn't get out and operate. We had a limited number of days to use the Falcon. She had to go back to New London and operate with the submarines and our date was set and firm; we had to be finished with her on a given date. The day before our last day with the Falcon it cleared enough to let us get out to sea far enough to get in 420 feet of water, and I made a dive from the Falcon to the bottom in 420 feet of water. That was the deepest dive that had ever been made at that time in the open sea.

Then we had to get out of there and get back in, get our gear and stuff off the Falcon and drop them at New London, and we went back to Washington.

We were still doing more work with the helium and oxygen and perfecting the equipment, working on the recompression tables, and on the 23rd day of May 1939, about 10:00 o'clock in the morning, we got word that a submarine was down just outside of Portsmouth, New Hampshire, for us to stand by with our personnel and equipment for orders. We would probably be ordered to the area as soon as more details were learned.

So we began to get what meager equipment we had together and ready for shipment. We didn't know how we were going to get up there, if we had to go. Some of the men rushed home and got a change of clothes, packed a small bag, and things, and sure enough, about 11:00 o'clock it was determined that the submarine was down and there were men aboard—all hands were aboard, but some of the men were alive—and for the experimental unit, equipment and personnel, to get to the scene of operations as soon as possible.

Q: This was the Squalus?

Chief Badders: That was the Squalus.*

Three other men and I took quite a bit of the equipment over to the Anacostia Naval Air Station, and we caught a Marine Reserve amphibious plane from there and flew into Portsmouth. We got in that evening.

Momsen, Dr. Yarbrough, and Dr. Behnke and some other divers had taken another plane and got in a little ahead of us.**

We arrived at the yard that evening, and by this time it was determined that there were 33 men alive aboard in the forward part of the submarine, but they hadn't been able to make any communication with anyone in the after part. They weren't sure whether there was anyone alive back there or not.

---

*USS Squalus (SS-192), commissioned in March 1939, began a series of test dives off Portsmouth, New Hampshire, in May of that year. On 23 May, failure of the main induction valve caused flooding in her aft engine room and she sank stern first to the bottom.
**Lieutenant Oscar D. Yarbrough, MC, USN; Lieutenant Albert R. Behnke, MC, USN.

Q: How deep was she?

Chief Badders: In 242 feet of water.

We got our equipment in operating condition and were transported by fast boat out to the sister ship of the Squalus, the Sculpin, standing by out there, and we were waiting for the Falcon. She was in New London, Connecticut, and she was speeding to the scene of operations as fast as she could with men and equipment and the rescue chamber. She arrived sometime early in the morning and got in position for diving operations. All of us people who had come down from Washington left the Sculpin and went aboard the Falcon.

Of course, the first order of business was to see what could be done about the men who were trapped in the submarine. They had broken the telephone cable on the buoy that was released internally from the submarine. The Sculpin had picked it up, and it drifted away with the buoy too far and put a strain on the cable and broke, so the only communication was through oscillators and people hammering on the hull. But before the telephone cable had broken, Lieutenant Naquin, the captain of the submarine, had told the commanding officer of the Sculpin that he had 33 men up there and he was unable to communicate with anyone aft. He didn't know whether anyone aft was alive or not, but he knew there were 33 men alive in the forward torpedo room and all in good shape.*

This buoy cable being broken loose from the Sculpin left us with no means of knowing just exactly where the submarine was. The Coast Guard was out, and one of their boats was dragging grapnels around and he hit the grapnel into her. They plumbed that up and down and indicated where the ship was. When the Falcon planted her moorings, they were planted around this area, of course, and then that line was used as the down line for the first dive that was made. The first business, of course, was for a diver to go down and hook up the down-haul wire and the rescue chamber, the wire that pulls the chamber down through the hatch to rescue survivors.

Sibitsky, one of the divers on the Falcon, made the first dive.** He went down this line, and after he hit the bottom, just a second or two after he reached the bottom, he said, "You're not going to believe this, but this grapnel hook is caught in the railing not more than 3 or 4 feet from the forward hatch of the Squalus, where we have to take the men out."

It couldn't have been placed any better if a diver had gone down and put it there himself.

So the down-haul wire was shackled on with this grapnel line and lowered to Sibitsky and he hooked the down-haul wire up all in one dive and came up. The rescue chamber was put in the water

---
*Lieutenant Oliver F. Naquin, USN.
**Boatswain's Mate Second Class Martin C. Sibitsky, USN.

ready for operations. The crew went aboard to operate it, a diver by the name of Harman and my later partner, operator Mihalowski, were the first two operators for the first trip. The chamber went down, and everything worked fine. We had had previous drills and all. And they brought seven men to the surface.

Q: The chamber could accommodate that number at one time?

Chief Badders: That's what it was designed for, seven passengers and two operators.

I was put in the chamber for the second trip with Harman, and I got to thinking on the way down I had operated this chamber probably more than anyone else in the Navy and I knew that it could handle more than seven men. On the way down to the hatch, I decided that I was going to bring more than seven men out on my trip, for the simple reason that if we only brought seven men out at a time, it was going to require a fifth trip to get all the men out. I knew that they could be brought out in four trips if a man or two extra was brought out in the other trips.

Q: Was oxygen inside becoming an urgent thing?

Chief Badders: No, no. In the rescue chamber there was atmospheric pressure all the time. There was fresh air circulating.

Q: No, I mean within the submarine, so it became imperative to get them out.

Chief Badders: Oh, no. There was no apparent danger to the men. The first trip down, fresh air was circulated through the compartment from the rescue chamber. Clothing, blankets, food, and things of that kind were given to them. The only danger that we thought about was that there's always the possibility of a bulkhead carrying away or something and flooding that area, or gas getting in.

My concern was to get the men out of there as soon as we could because---fortunately, in this operation we had good weather at that time, but there's always a possibility of one of those crazy squalls coming up that they have in that area and having to run to get away with men alive on the bottom.

So on my first trip, I brought nine men up. I hadn't said a word to anybody on topside about it, but I came up with the nine men with no difficulty at all, unloaded them, still hadn't said anything. Of course, they're counting these men when they get out of this chamber on the deck of the *Falcon*. We unloaded them out of the chamber on the deck of the *Falcon*, and a doctor would examine them real quick. Then they'd load them up and take them to the hospital in Portsmouth.

Well, I was also going to make the third trip in the chamber, and I knew that when I made the second trip. I got the men out of there as soon as I could, dogged the hatch down, and got started down again. I think it was Momsen who said to me on the phone, "You brought out too many men on that trip, but do it again and bring up nine the next time." So I brought nine up on the second trip, which left only two trips required to bring the rest of the men up. I brought 18 men out of there, out of that sunken submarine. There are their autographs on the wall, on that list of survivors.

Well, on the fourth trip, the operators went down to bring the last survivors out, and on the way up the chamber got fouled up in the down-haul wiring. The down-haul wire got in the gears of the drum somehow or other and fouled the chamber. It couldn't go up or down, so we had quite a time getting that chamber-load to the surface. It took three or four hours to get them up. We had to send a diver down to cut the down-haul wire loose at the submarine, and the chamber had to be pulled up very carefully, because if it came up too fast it could displace water out of the ballast tank and cause some damage or something.

The next day, after all the survivors were off, Admiral Cole, who was the admiral in charge of the operations—he was commandant of the Portsmouth Navy Yard at the time—said, "We've got to determine if there's any life left aft in the submarine. It will require a trip of the rescue chamber, open the hatch aft, and determine for sure if the after part of the submarine is flooded or dry.*

Well, some overhaul work had to be done on the chamber to replace this down-haul wire and everything, and they waited until the next morning. They did this work during the night, and the next morning Mihalowski and I were selected to make this so-called fifth trip with the rescue chamber to the after hatch. The down-haul wire was hooked up, and Mike and I got in the chamber and down we went.

To make this trip, the chamber had to be secured over the hatch and then pressure built up in the chamber equivalent to bottom pressure; otherwise if you unscrewed that hatch and the after part of the submarine was flooded at 240 feet of depth, and the rescue chamber was under atmospheric pressure, the water would have come right up out of the submarine into the rescue chamber.

So we had to sit the chamber down in place over the hatch, dog it down with the holding-down bolts, and then build a pressure up in the chamber equivalent to bottom pressure. That meant that Mike and I were in the chamber with pressure built up to 240 feet aft and bolted to the submarine with bolts internal. If we had become incapacitated or passed out from compressed air, we'd have been hooked up down there just like the men in the

---
*Rear Admiral Cyrus W. Cole, USN.

submarine and no way of getting us out. But fortunately nothing happened.

We got everything all set and let the pressure build up, then opened the hatch and, sure enough, when I first partially undogged the hatch a gush of air came out of the submarine into the rescue chamber. I was down in the lower compartment of the rescue chamber handling the hatch. Mihalowski was handling the valves, pressure gauges, and all in the top compartment, and he hadn't built up quite enough pressure; otherwise the air wouldn't have come out. As soon as he built up a little more pressure in the rescue chamber, the air stopped coming in, and I opened the hatch the rest of the way and it was flooded right up to the neck of the hatch, which indicated there couldn't possibly be any life down there.

We made a report to the topside, dogged the hatch down, released the rescue chamber, and came on to the surface.

That indicated that rescue operations were finished and it was strictly a salvage operation in bringing the submarine up, which we did. We went to work on it with pontoons, drying as many compartments as practical with ballast tanks and whatnot, and raised her. That's a long story of salvage and I don't think you want me to go into too many details of this. I think everybody's read about the salvage of the Squalus.*

Q: Yes.

Chief Badders: She was successfully raised.

Q: That must have been a thrill, though, to rescue the 33 men.

Chief Badders: Oh, you know, the first thing I thought of when I made my first trip with survivors, when I opened that hatch and the first couple of men came out of that submarine into the rescue chamber---the first thing that entered my mind was, boy, just why couldn't we have had this when we had those six men alive in the S-4. They had to finally die down there because we had no way of getting them out. If we'd just had that rescue chamber then, we could have saved those six men just as easily as we saved the 33 on the Squalus, in fact much easier because she was only down in 102 feet of water. And we should have had that chamber then because things of that kind had been suggested after the S-51 job, but absolutely nothing was done about it. I'm not blaming the Navy for this, because the Navy can only do what it has the money to do and time to do it, and there just wasn't

---

*See Edward Parks, "Fate Toyed with Squalus Crew on 19th Dive," Navy Times, 3 March 1986, pages 10, 32, and 36. The article is accompanied by paintings which depict the rescue chamber and its attachment to the submarine.

anyone interested in giving us the money and time to develop things of that kind.

Q: Mr. Badders, with the use of helium and oxygen, what has become the maximum depth for a diver?

Chief Badders: I was just reading in this magazine that there were two men down 1,600 feet for something like 10 or 12 hours. They have gone into now, of course, what they call total saturation. It's supposed to be new, that is in the last two or three years they've gone into it extensively, but we knew that we could do that back in 1938. We knew that the human body would only absorb so much gas, and then it wouldn't absorb any more regardless of what depth the diver was or what pressure he was under or how long he stayed there. We had more or less accidentally discovered that, and it was familiar, but we didn't pursue that procedure.

It became apparent from these deep oil well operations and some of these things that required diving operations that men had to go deep and stay a long time to get anything done. We needed some operating procedure that could prevent this short time on the bottom and extensive time in decompression, which made these operations cost so much money that they were impractical. So they began to experiment with this total saturation thing. They'd put a diver down, for instance, to 300 feet and leave him there until he had absorbed all the gas that his system would absorb, and then he could stay there for a week or two, 10-15 days or longer, for that matter, without absorbing any more gas.

In other words, from that time on decompression time wouldn't change coming up appreciably. So that's the way they're working it now. They're going down and they have a job to do in, say, 200 feet of water and the men are totally saturated on the surface before they go down in chambers. Then they go down in a pressurized chamber, open the chamber, and whatever type of diving equipment they're going to use for the job, work six or eight hours, if they want to, or whatever the work requires, and back into the chamber, bring them to the surface and hook them up to the dry chamber on the surface, keep it under the same pressure all the time, feed them, change clothes, whatever. And while they're up another team of divers is down under the same conditions. They keep rotating in that manner until whatever job they're on is completed. Then they go into the long-drawn-out decompression requirements on the surface to bring them back to normal pressure.

Q: Do temperatures become a factor at these great depths?

Chief Badders: Very definitely, but the Navy and civilian concerns have developed means of keeping the divers warm electrically. I think they're still in the electrical field, but mostly circulating warm water through a part of the clothing that they wear, heating elements that keep the water at different temperatures required for the bottom to keep them warm. The deep-submergence outfits on the West Coast, the Navy's Sealab is a total saturation thing. They go down 15 days or more out there.

Q: For the individual diver does the underwater life constitute an obstacle of any kind?

Chief Badders: You mean detrimental to the health in the future?

Q: Well, I mean to the effectiveness of his operations as a diver? Sea life, sea creatures, what have you?

Chief Badders: Oh, no, they haven't been bothered in any way. There are a lot of wild stories, mostly fictional, about divers being attacked by manta rays and sharks and things of that kind, but actually I don't know of one case where it actually happened, where a diver was attacked by a shark or manta rays or anything of that kind. An octopus will wrap around a guy once in a while, I guess, if he gets around a big one, but that's no problem. They can cut themselves loose or get away somehow. We've had no real casualties in that way; that's for sure.

Q: About the time you were talking about, the French diver, Piccard, was operating, was he not?* Did we learn anything from his operations that was useful to us?

Chief Badders: I think the most we learned from him was how to build pressurized vessels to keep men under atmospheric pressure and put them down for observation at great depths.

Q: He had his bathysphere?

Chief Badders: Right, and from that have come these high-pressurized units that are going down 15,000 or 20,000 feet now. I think that's an offshoot from his original exploratory work.

The work that he could do from the inside of a vessel of that type was very limited. The fact of the matter is I don't believe he had any means of performing any task other than observation. It could be used for directing operations from topside, for instance, lowering explosives and putting them in the proper place, things of that kind, or hooks to hook into objects on the bottom and things of that kind.

Since the time of his first work in that line, they have developed mechanical arms and things that they are using pretty

---

*Auguste Piccard and his son Jacques established a world record, since broken, for descent into the sea when they took a bathyscaphe to more than 10,000 feet below the surface in the late 1940s.

successfully for a lot of different tasks on the bottom. My understanding is that the Navy is working right now on units of that kind that will be almost purely mechanical; there will be no outside help at all from the diving angle. All the work will be done from inside of a pressurized—pressure-proof—vessel through mechanical means of electronics and mechanically-operated arms. They're doing great things.

Q: So the individual diver will not have to operate outside the lab?

Chief Badders: Not at great depths. I'm speaking of depths of 10,000, 15,000, 20,000 feet. I don't believe the time will ever come that we're going to get divers down and perform any useful tasks out in the water any deeper than 1,000 feet. I don't believe it's going to work. Things are happening to human bodies that have been exposed to these pressures, and it just hasn't been determined yet what these effects are going to be in the future on a man's system.

For instance, not long ago a man was down over here in Washington in a normal dive; it was 200, 300, or 400 feet. He came up and everything was supposed to be perfectly normal, but the man is stone deaf. He never has regained his hearing, and the last I heard of it there is no indication why he had gone deaf. His eardrums weren't ruptured, nothing that they found.

It had to be some action on the nerves, I suppose, but it didn't show up on examination. He was stone deaf, and it still seems he'll be permanently deaf--a chief petty officer with about 18 years' service.

Q: During your period of activity as a diver, were there any limitations on the length of time that a man could normally engage in diving? Was there anything of this sort that began to develop?

Chief Badders: No. We had no real permanent effects on anyone. Practically all of us had the bends from these experimental tables we were running. You couldn't tell how far a table would go until you went to its limit and saw what would happen, and sometimes we would get the bends. I had the bends several times pretty severely, but proper decompression and recompression overcame it and, as far as I know, I don't have any effects from any of that. I have a very bad shoulder and neck right now in the area where I was hit the most often and the hardest with the bends, and I sometimes wonder if that didn't have some effect on my condition now, but any doctors that I've talked to say no, it's something else. So during my work we had no aftereffects that amounted to anything at all. Nothing that wasn't cured in time.

We had one man who went into shock and he was not in bad

shape, but some of his faculties didn't work the way they should for a couple of months. But he eventually recovered, totally recovered, as far as the doctors could determine.

Q: So, unlike an athlete who has a limited period of time for his profession, the diver isn't limited in this way at all?

Chief Badders: Not time so much, but age. During my time—and I think it's still in effect—first class and master divers, when they become 40 years old, are automatically disqualified for deep diving, but they can be waivered. Those regulations can be waivered if he is still in physical condition to go ahead. That happened to me. While I was still in Washington I was 40, and agewise I was supposed to be disqualified, but the doctors found me in excellent physical condition. You had to be examined every three months, once a quarter, to make sure that you stayed in that condition.

Q: What is the thinking behind a regulation like that? Why 40 as the cutoff date?

Chief Badders: I really don't know. It's like everything else in the Navy. If something weighs a certain amount and a certain sized wire will lift it, well, we'll use a wire twice that big to do it for safety. So I think maybe a man might go to 50 or 60 years old and still be all right, if he's physically all right, but the Navy says, well, it can be done that far, but let's make it safe and cut it off at 40, which, in some cases, takes men out of service that are right in their prime, if the regulation was pushed without his waiver thing.

I don't know if that waiver is still in effect or not, but I believe it is because I see men around Washington that I'm pretty sure are over 40 years old. At least they're instructing and making some dives. I suppose that the doctors figure when a man gets 40 he has begun to deteriorate and he shouldn't speed up the process. I know in my case I felt, and it was proved by all the physical exams that they could give me when I was 40 years old, I was in as good shape as I was in my 20s--I felt as good or better.

Q: And you had much more experience and wisdom to emply.

Chief Badders: Right.

Q: How long did you continue to dive, actually?

Chief Badders: Of course, I wasn't doing any deep diving in the Panama Canal, but I was diving not too regularly but regularly enough up until the time I retired when I was 62 years old. Of course, there again, as I say, diving down there was shallow diving, mostly ships' hull inspections and some construction work that would take you down maybe 60 or 75 feet.

I had one job in the Panama Canal that came up a couple of times, one of the dams that required diving to 120 feet. That was the deepest we ever had in the Panama Canal. I was considered to be in very good condition when I retired in the canal. Down there you have to retire when you're 62 years old. I knew I was good for five or six more years in my job down there, but there again somebody said age is age, and that's it regardless of who you are. Like my automobile out there. I've got a 1968 automobile that's a better automobile than a lot of 1971s that are running around today, and it's the way I've taken care of it, and the way I take care of myself has to do with my physical condition.

Q: You said that Admiral Cole had the *Squalus* put in dry dock on your birthday in Portsmouth.

Chief Badders: Well, previous to that we had had quite a problem of getting a line under the stern of the *Squalus* to get the chains in position for the pontoons. It was too deep for the tunneling operation that had been done on the *S-51* and *S-4* jobs for working the chains under, and we were trying to work a line under the stern with a lance, a combination of water and air being forced under the submarine. As I say, we had quite a lot of trouble with this thing and had consumed an awful lot of time, and the day that we finally completed the operation, the lance completely circled the stern, under from one side and up on the other side, and we knew we were going to get a line under the boat, happened to be the morning of Admiral Cole's birthday. He hadn't come out to the operation that morning, so I sent in a message to him, a personal message myself, congratulating him on his birthday---I forget what birthday it was now, but he was getting up in age and retired right after the Squalus job---and said the lance is completely around the submarine, we'll have lines under it by tomorrow, and signed it Bill Badders.* He was so pleased with that and when we got the submarine in it was supposed to arrive on the 14th and he said, "I want to get that thing in dry dock tomorrow, on your birthday." It turned out that there was a lot of work to do to get the submarine itself ready and the dry dock, mostly work on the submarine, getting the pontoons off of her and getting her on an even keel and in proper trim for going in on the blocks. So we had to work real late that evening so as to be sure and get her in on the next day, the 15th of September, which would be on my birthday, so that was my birthday present from Admiral Cole.

---

*Cole was born 21 June 1876.

Badders #3 - 101

Interview Number 3 with Chief Machinist's Mate William Badders,
U.S. Navy (Retired)

Place: Chief Badders's home in Annapolis, Maryland

Date: Monday morning, 8 November 1971

Subject: Biography

Interviewer: John T. Mason, Jr.

Q: It's good to see you again this morning, Mr. Badders. Last time, you gave me that most interesting account of the rescue from the Squalus and you concluded your remarks at that time with the dry-docking of the Squalus on the 15th of September 1939. Do you want to resume the story from that point?

Chief Badders: A couple of days after the Squalus was placed in dry dock, our group, the experimental diving unit group, left the Portsmouth, New Hampshire, area and returned to our duty station at the experimental diving unit in Washington, D.C. We had two or three weeks' work getting our equipment cleaned up and overhauled and back in working order that we had used on the Squalus.

Q: And the inevitable reports, too, I suppose?

Chief Badders: Yes, miles and miles of reports to be made. Rough logs had been kept, of course, of every activity and every phase of the operation. That all had to be smoothed out and shortened up for the bureaus concerned, and that took time. So we really didn't accomplish much the rest of the year in the line of diving.

We had made the two deep dives previous to the Squalus disaster, and it was determined that we wouldn't go that deep again with the equipment available at the experimental unit. The diving tank wasn't built for that pressure, so we had gone as deep as we could . . .

Q: That being 500 feet?

Chief Badders: Five hundred feet, right, and it was a matter of perfecting some of the tools and some of the procedures that we had inaugurated on the Squalus job, smoothing some of them out and getting them ready to be approved by the bureaus and adopted as standard procedures and standard pieces of equipment for future use in the Navy. It didn't take long for the end of the year to come along. In the meantime, there were ceremonies in the Navy Department and different places, different men were decorated for different phases of the operation. The divers received Navy Crosses late in the fall, and I guess it was sometime in late November or early December that we got the word that four of us were definitely going to be decorated sometime in the near future with the Congressional Medal of Honor. Of course, that put us on edge. That was pretty great.

On the ninth of January 1940, McDonald, Mihalowski, Crandall, and myself went to the White House and received our Congressional Medals of Honor for the work that we had done in the rescue and salvage operations on the Squalus.*

By this time the war was inevitable and we were sure we were . . .

Q: And the presentation was made by the President?

Chief Badders: Right, President Roosevelt.

Q: Can you recall the incident?

Chief Badders: Well, the incident at the White House didn't amount to very much, because the President was not well. He was very ill, and we didn't even have the news media or photographers there. He presented the medals and shook hands with us and gave us a little pat on the back, and from there we went to the Secretary of the Navy's office in the old Navy Building and then the whole thing was done all over again with him presenting the medals with the news media and the newsreel cameras and all of that. That's this picture over here on the wall, the

---
*The other Medal of Honor winners were Chief Metalsmith James H. McDonald, USN; Torpedoman First Class John Mihalowski, USN; and Chief Boatswain's Mate Orson L. Crandall, USN.

Secretary of the Navy hanging the medal around my neck.

Q: Who was the Secretary of the Navy?

Chief Badders: It was Edison.*

So we began to work with different gas mixtures, making different dives, and testing our recompression tables, and whatnot. Several of the men were transferred to other activities. Two or three of them, the so-called guinea pig crowd, the personnel attached to the experimental unit were sent out to different billets. New men came in.

I got the word that the Panama Canal wanted a master diver-salvage master. At that time I was a senior master diver in the Navy, and they anticipated sending me to the Panama Canal for the job that they wanted to set up for the war effort there. Well, I figured that I wasn't going to be around Washington very much longer; I'd be at the Panama Canal. Sure enough, in early March 1940 it was determined that they wouldn't send me down there on active duty. The governor of the Panama Canal, being an Army general under the Army Engineer Corps, wanted a man there that no other branch of military service would have any jurisdiction over. In other words, when he got a man there, he wanted to be sure he was going to keep him there. He didn't want

---

*Charles Edison, son of inventor Thomas Edison, was Secretary of the Navy from January to June 1940.

naval orders to come in transferring him away about the time he got an organization set up.

Q: One would be under Civil Service then?

Chief Badders: Right. So they transferred me from the regular Navy--at that time I had 22-1/2 years of active duty--to the Fleet Reserve, which put me in a civilian status and, of course, still subject to naval orders.

Q: How did you feel about that change of status?

Chief Badders: At the time it was going on, I was very enthusiastic about it all. I thought, "Gee, this is great. I'm going out here with 22 years' service. I'm going to draw my 22-year Fleet Reserve pay, and I'm going to draw a salary from the Panama Canal." In the meantime, I'm going to be doing something real great for the war effort, if things go on the way it had been explained up to then.

Q: You didn't mind the idea of the Panama Canal?

Chief Badders: Oh, no, I had no regret about being considered for this. In fact, I thought it was quite an honor.

I went through all this procedure and went into the Fleet

Reserve on the 12th day of March, left New York City the 13th day of March for the Panama Canal. There wasn't a day lapse of service between active duty in the Navy and on the payroll of the Panama Canal.

Q: Did you take your family with you?

Chief Badders: Not at that time. My family couldn't go down there until I had been on the job long enough to provide quarters for them. All employees of the Panama Canal had to live in what they called Panama Canal Government quarters, and people were coming in there by the thousands for new construction projects for the defense of the canal and so on, which meant that the place just didn't have quarters available for everybody immediately that went in there. That was the only unpleasant thing about the whole deal.

Immediately upon my arrival at the canal, they laid out the program that they had in mind. They wanted a diving organization---diving and salvage organization---to keep the Panama Canal open under any conditions. If we had ships bombed or lock gates damaged by bombing or sabotage or ships ramming or anything of that kind, we had to make immediate repairs and keep this thing open. The governor told me at the time, "Put in simple words, your job is to keep this canal open from Buoy 1 Atlantic to Buoy 1 Pacific. Whatever it takes to do that, you have the funds and the backing of the organization here to get the people and equipment to get ready for it."

Q: I take it there wasn't any such organization in being then.

Chief Badders: The only divers in the Panama Canal was one diver at each set of locks to do minor repair work in the locks---pick up things that were dropped in the lock chambers, unplug valves that were jammed up, and things of that kind. I guess there were about four or five divers in the whole Panama Canal.

Q: Were they Navy divers?

Chief Badders: No, they were civilian divers, employees of the Panama Canal, and they were so far behind they were still using the old hand pump system of diving, men turning the hand pumps cranking air down to them. This was in 1940, and that's how far behind they were.

Q: What had they done in the case of a real salvage job?

Chief Badders: They hadn't had a real salvage job in the canal up to then. They just hadn't had anything other than groundings, and they don't require much diving generally. It's a matter of pulling and tugging and getting the thing floating again, unless the ship is damaged, has a hole knocked in it when it went aground. But they hadn't had any problems like that down there.

By this time they were having all this bombing over in Europe, plugging up harbors and stuff of that kind, and they didn't want it to happen in the canal. They just couldn't have it happen, because in addition to the Navy ships going through the canal both ways, the merchant ships, tankers, and troopships and things of that kind just had to get through. Otherwise, as you know, they'd have to go all the way around the point and it would take days and days longer to transport material and people.

So I went to work drawing up a plan, and when I'd finished with it, it was approved. My first main function was to establish a diving school. You couldn't hire divers. There weren't any available anywhere by that time. I had to build a diving school, make up the curriculum, designate the qualifications of the candidates for the diving school, and so on. That was all approved not only by the Panama Canal, but my curriculum was sent to the Navy Department and the Navy approved of it to the extent that they allowed me to use the same curriculum putting Navy people through my school in the Panama Canal, if and when we had space available and the time to train them. And I did; I trained over 100 Navy men down there and made salvage or second class divers out of them.

Q: How many men did you feel that you needed for your project?

Chief Badders: We figured we were going to need about 50 men on hand at all times to be absolutely safe, which I never did reach---never did reach 50. I put a class of people through---let me go back to establishing the school, first, before I go into that.

We had to have a lot of equipment, air compressors, welding machines, pumps, and things of that kind, and by this time these things were hard to get. There was high priority on them for other purposes all over the world. And the Normandie turned over at Pier 88 in New York, and that was a major salvage operation.*

Q: Indeed it was.

Chief Badders: I went sent up there as an observer on that job and to be associated with, at that time, Commander Sullivan, who was in charge of that operation, and get a line on the equipment that would be most suitable for our operations in the Panama Canal.** I was there about six weeks, I guess, running from

---

*The French luxury liner, SS Normandie, was seized and interned in New York at the outbreak of World War II. In December 1941 she was designated as a Navy transport and renamed USS Lafayette (AP-53). During conversion she caught fire on 9 February 1942 and as the result of a chaotic and poorly planned fire-fighting effort, she was overloaded with water, keeled over and sank at her slip. The Lafayette was righted in August 1943 and reclassified APV-4, but had been so extensively damaged that plans to complete conversion were stopped. After the war she was sold to a New Jersey company for scrap.

**Commander William A. Sullivan, USN. Sullivan's oral history is in the Columbia University collection.

there all over the United States to different manufacturers of pumps and welding machines, picking up what we could for the canal. Sullivan helped us a lot by allotting quite a bit of the Navy-procured equipment that he transferred to us.

Well, I got back to the canal and my diving school building was about completed. I was building the school on the banks of Gatun Lake, right adjacent to the only ship that had ever sunk in the Panama Canal. She was lying on the bottom right at that area, a little old combination freighter and passenger ship that somehow started leaking coming through the canal. They ran it over against the bank, and it turned over and slid down to the bottom. They never did anything about bringing it up, so I thought that would be an ideal place for a training ground for training divers.

In the meantime, before I left to go to New York, I had drawn up the qualifications a man would have to have to enter the diving school. He had to be under 30 years of age. He would have to be a man who had completed an apprenticeship and served at least a year in his trade, and the trades that were more apt to be used underwater, such as welders, burners, riggers, shipwrights, carpenters, machinists, pipefitters, shipfitters, those ratings. When I came back, I had over 300 applications on my desk to sieve through for people who met that much of the qualifications.

Q: Where were these people?

Chief Badders: All over the Panama Canal. All the employees of the Panama Canal, the different shops and activities of the Panama Canal.

Q: Oh, they were all there, within the family, so to speak?

Chief Badders: Oh, yes. All the men were already employed by the Panama Canal, but the ones that I selected would be transferred to me for each class that I ran.

Q: And what was the inducement for them? Was it higher pay?

Chief Badders: Slightly higher pay than they were making in the shops. Oh, I'd say a half more. And I suppose it was considered a kind of glamorous job at times, interesting at least.

As I said, I considered that I wanted about 50 men available who were qualified divers, and I set my curriculum up originally so that it would be about a three-month course of instruction. By this time the war was really going. Pearl Harbor had been hit by the time I finally got the diving school and everything all organized. So they said, "Well, we can't take three months to make divers. We've got to have some men that can do something in a shorter period of time than that. What are you going to do about it?"

I said, "Well, I'll take a class with the equipment I have and the personnel I had on hand." I figured I could handle 12 divers, and I trained the diver tenders at the same time. By the way, the diver tenders were supposed to have been apprentice boys, men who were in the apprentice program for the canal.

Q: Would you define a diver tender? What is he?

Chief Badders: He's the man that dresses the diver and tends his lifeline and air hose while he's on the bottom, takes care of his equipment, and assists him by getting the tools to him that he requires, taking care of things topside, watching the air compressor and---if welding machines are used---the welders and all that business.

Q: The diver's Man Friday!

Chief Badders: Right. In other words, a very good candidate for a diver in the future, and that was the reason I had taken the apprentice boys, hoping that they would continue on as tenders and eventually get out of the apprenticeship program and then they would be available for the diving program. But this never happened. These apprentice boys were all subject to draft, and as fast as I could get a group of them through the school the next thing I knew they'd all be gone on the draft. So it wasn't very long until I saw that that end of the program wasn't going to work at all. I had to get away from the apprentice boy idea and use what we called the local rate people for tenders, the Panamanian laborers. I had a choice of the very best caliber of Panamanian laborers like welder helpers and rigger helpers and carpenter helpers and things of that kind. They were the people I called in.

Q: How did they compare with the others?

Chief Badders: There wasn't any comparison. You can't compare any Panamanian laborer with any American boy who's smart enough to be an apprentice boy in the apprentice program down there. The Panamanian laborer was one of the big headaches as far as I was concerned all the time I was in the Panama Canal, and I guess still is.

Q: You mean they just don't have the qualifications?

Chief Badders: That's right. They're illiterate, to start with, and they have a saturation point. You can teach them just so much, and when you hit that point, you just can't ever beat anything else into their thick skulls. They just can't absorb it. That's all there is to it.

Q: Are they largely of Indian origin?

Chief Badders: Everything, and about 80% of them are illegitimate people to begin with, as you know, the Panamanian general public. Some Indian, some Jamaicans, Colombians, Panamanians. They not only are not as smart, of course, as the American boys, but they wouldn't be dependable in any real emergency, and that's where you need some action, somebody who can think for himself. If a diver got in really serious trouble all of a sudden, they'd just go all to pieces and couldn't do anything. Some of the American people, divers or anyone who happened to be around the operation on the topside would have to take over and do the job.

Q: I would think, faced with that problem and if the authorities realized it, some sort of protection from the draft could have been obtained?

Chief Badders: They attempted that, but the boys themselves wanted to go, and that's where 80% of my divers went. They'd get through the diving school and go back to their shop. You see, the setup was the men would go through the diving school, and if they successfully completed the course of instruction, they were rated a diver; they had a dual rate. Say a man's a machinist, he'd be a diver and machinist. Well, when he wasn't diving, he'd be working in the shop as a machinist. If I had a job that required a machinist's ability under water, I'd call him out from the machine shop to my organization as a diver. And then immediately he'd go on diving pay until that operation was finished, and he went back to the shop.

But many, many of these people, of course, were young men. They were all under 30, and I don't know how many of them went into the Seabees from down there, and a lot of them made out real well. They became good divers in the Seabee operations. A lot of them just quit diving altogether when they went in the Seabees and operated heavy equipment and became welders and all that kind of thing.

Q: But your operation was equally as vital to the war effort as were the Seabees?

Chief Badders: Right, but you couldn't stop a man if he wanted to go and enlist in the Seabees or something. There was no way to stop him from doing it; away he went, which put me in a bight in this respect. When they said, "Well, we've got to have some divers who can do something and get them quick," I said, "Okay, I've got my curriculum down to six weeks, and I'll put three classes through, 12 men. The first class six weeks, the second class six weeks, the third class six weeks, then I'll call the first class back for a second six weeks and go on from there and advance them that much more." Well, I never did get the first class back, and I must have run 50 classes through during the war, because they would be dwindled down to where I just wouldn't have them available to come back for advanced training.

Q: That was a pretty discouraging operation!

Chief Badders: Yes! It really put me under a handicap. But these men were exceptionally good men, and we had a lot of underwater construction work in the canal, and these men were doing that work.

Q: What kind of construction?

Chief Badders: Piers and docks and dams, pipelines, and all that kind of thing. They ran three huge pipelines all the way across the isthmus, you know. They could pull a tanker in the Atlantic side and pump oil right into a tanker in the Pacific without putting the ships through the canal. That went through Gatun Lake and part of the canal. That took quite a lot of diving.

We gained experience all the time and were getting better and better. In the meantime, we were having things happen; ships were getting in trouble, by this time. The longer the war went on, the worse the ships became, not only mechnically, but it seemed that the people who were operating the ships—if it hadn't been for the war, they wouldn't have made good able-bodied seamen and they'd be up there as a skipper or chief mate or something operating the ship, and you never knew what was going to happen. We had a lot of groundings. Fortunately, nothing serious happened in the lock chambers. No gates were rammed or anything of that kind because the pilots, of course, had control. But they had control in the reaches and in the lake, too, for that matter, but things would happen—mechanical failures, steering gear failures. A pilot would holler for so many degrees right rudder and he'd get twice that many degrees left rudder, and in a canal that narrow you don't have much time to correct that and you ground, and good and hard, if you're making eight or ten knots. A ship would go aground, and I'd have to get all of my facilities out there and get that thing out. Sometimes it would require partially unloading the ship, sometimes bringing the big dipper dredges out and dredging part of the mud alongside, put tugs on her and pull beach gear, any way to get them afloat, and if they weren't damaged, well, that would be the end of that. But if the ship had a hole in it from going aground, which some of them did—they didn't only hit soft mud—that had to be patched up, and in some cases it had to be patched well enough to get them into dry dock down there and make permanent repairs. In other cases we made repairs that were strong enough and permanent enough to get them on to their destination, the South Pacific or wherever.

I wouldn't even hazard a guess at how many ships we had aground and damaged. In Culebra Cut they'd hit the bank, and when they hit that they invariably knocked holes in the side. We never had one that was damaged enough that it sank in that area. We were always able to get it into some beaching zone where we could run it aground and it wouldn't sink any deeper, and make repairs to the damage.

We were kept pretty busy. In addition to trying to keep up with my new divers, keep enough divers on hand---I never did really have enough---and then doing these jobs when they came up. And that's another thing. When these jobs would come up while I had a class going in school, I'd take everybody right from the school, all the student divers. I'd take them right to that job and use them as much as I could on the job. At least they would be there and see how things were going on, and that period of time would not be considered a part of their six weeks' training because I wouldn't be at the school to handle them during that period anyway.

Q: Did you do all the instructing?

Chief Badders: I had two assistants who took care of some of the instructing, but I did most of it. I was a pretty busy boy, 12 hours a day, seven days a week down there for about two and a half years.

Q: What kind of administrative staff did you have to back you up?

Chief Badders: I had my own secretaries and timekeepers and whatnot. Then my big bookkeeping expenditures of funds and all that kind of business went through what we called at that time the mechanical division offices down there. They just took my budget and my program and all my big letter-writing and things of that kind went through their office. That was the division that had shipyards, the mechanical division of the shipyards, a big yard on the Pacific and one on the Atlantic side. The offices at the Atlantic end did most of my work, and I came directly under the Navy captain who was in charge of the mechnical division. We called him mechanical division superintendent. During the war it was old Captain Kiernan, a fine old man, an old MIT graduate.*

Q: On average, how many ships went through the canal a day?

Chief Badders: It varied. To hit an average I wouldn't even hazard a guess. You see, what would happen was they'd come in there in convoys, and if they were coming from the Atlantic and going to the Pacific they would bring in maybe 50 ships in a convoy. Then they would refuel, resupply, whatever they needed

---

*Captain James E. Kiernan, USN, Massachusetts Institute of Technology class of 1922.

in that area to get everything all set for the final run on to the South Pacific, and then they would run them through just one right after the other till they got them all through. Actually, they're putting more ships through the Panama Canal right now than we ever did in World War II, percentagewise today more tonnage, more numbers of ships. They have modernized the handling procedures and all that.

Q: Did you have any problem with the super-sized ships?

Chief Badders: We didn't have the super-sized ships then. The biggest tanker we had, about the biggest, was the T2 tanker.* We had some large carriers, and the large carriers and the large battleships were our biggest problem going through the canal, that is sizewise. But we rarely had any kind of a problem with them other than the tight squeeze in the locks and so on. One did some damage to the bow. I think they scraped the bank in Culebra Cut a bit and just wrinkled up some plates and caused some slight leaks. We had to do a lot of welding on it, welding up small cracks and things of that kind.

Q: The Queen Elizabeth also went through, didn't she?

---

*A T2 tanker was approximately 500 feet long with a beam of about 70 feet and draft of 40 feet.

Chief Badders: Yes, that was one of the big ones.

Our biggest headache was the old Liberty ships, Victory ships, and things of that kind. Darn those things, you never knew when one of them was going to break in two on you, and they seemed to have the most helter-skelter crews of any bunch of people I ever ran into. Then, of course, we had our foreign flags going through there, too, that caused us a lot of trouble. The English ships going through there.

Q: Why would they cause special trouble?

Chief Badders: They weren't special trouble, but when we had trouble with them it was generally real trouble. They would have some kind of mechanical failure. Their equipment was in such deplorable condition, they couldn't depend on it at all. They'd try to drop an anchor, and the anchor engine wouldn't work. Couldn't even drop an anchor on a ship one time, which meant that he just kept going, and before they could get the power they required and reverse, why, they barreled into the back end of the ship in front of them.

We had one Liberty ship--we had one convoy coming in the Atlantic end of the canal that was so large they didn't have enough pilots to put a pilot on every ship, so they put a pilot on every other ship, and the one in the middle that didn't have a pilot was supposed to watch the man in front of him and the man behind him and guide him in. Well, there came up one of the worst rainstorms that we'd had in years down there and, of course, the one in the middle just couldn't see the man in front of him at all--period. He couldn't even see the bow of his ship, and he got completely out of line and ran aground outside the breakwater. He went into Cristobal Harbor, and he ran aground good and hard on the rocks. The ship lay there and broke in two.

Q: These were filled with supplies, were they?

Chief Badders: Yes. This particular ship was loaded with drums of asphalt for runways and personnel carriers and jeeps, hundreds of them on the darned thing. We unloaded all the personnel carriers, jeeps, and things of that kind we could get off that were worth saving, put them in barges, and that's the last I ever saw of them. They went somewhere. And then we blasted the bow section apart and sank it in the mud. They always broke right forward of the forward fireroom bulkhead, and the after section was watertight. So I ordered it flooded to keep it from going farther aground, but once we pumped that out, the water that I had put in her to keep her stable, it wasn't much of a pull to get the stern section off the rocks. And we took that way outside in deep water and set a mine off in the bottom of her and sank it.

Badders #3 - 123

Q: What was the cause of this weakness that made the ships break in two?

Chief Badders: Some construction design that wasn't figured out, I guess, when they built them. I don't know, but that was the weak part of all that type ship.

Q: Was it reflected in the attitude of the crews?

Chief Badders: Yes, it was. For instance, this one that ran aground, when this thing started to break apart--it was so rough we couldn't get boats out to get the crew off, that is, with any kind of safety at all. You were taking a chance on sinking your boats and maybe losing the boat crew or something. So we left the men on board. Nothing can happen to them. The thing's aground, nothing else can happen although it's breaking in two and it's popping. If you ever hear a ship break in two, the plates breaking, it sounds like guns going off, you know. This thing was making a terrific noise and working, and the crew went nuts. They wanted to get off that ship, and they kept screaming and hollering that we were--it was close enough to the beach that you could hear them through bullhorns. So to calm their nerves and try to do something, the admiral was on the scene by this time, the commandant of the 15th Naval District, and was advising we've got to do something, we've got men out there.

I said, "Well, we can't get a boat out there with any safety. Those people are just crazy, but nothing can really happen to them. Even if the ship fell over on its side, they'd still be above water. They're high and dry. It's not bad."

And he said, "Can you rig a highline or something out there and bring them ashore on a breeches buoy?"

I said, "Well, it can be done." I had highline equipment, but how are you going to get a line out there? I made them bring a target-towing plane out, towing this target sleeve, and they dropped the sleeve over on the beach and when they crossed over the ship, dropped the wire off the plane like they drop these things on runways. The wire landed across the deck of the ship and the sleeve was ashore. Well, the minute I got that little old stinking wire from that ship to shore, those people calmed down. They knew then there's something over here and from that we'll get something else. And we never did put a breeches buoy out to get them off. They began to calm down; we could see that they were quieting down and weren't making so many demands for rescue.

The next morning, at daybreak, it had calmed down enough so we could get boats out from shore. Then some of them didn't come ashore; they stayed aboard for a day or two. But they really wanted to get off of that ship! They didn't know for sure what was happening. That's what it was. It was making so much noise in the dark, pouring down rain, just sheets of rain, and here this terrific tearing and ripping of steel plates, and they just thought that ship was disintegrating right under them, working, you know, on the rocks.

Q: They were panicked!

Chief Badders: Right. They were just panicked. There were a few there that weren't panicking, but there weren't enough in that group to keep the others under control and convince them that they were in good shape. That was one of my most interesting experiences. It lasted about three days before we could even do anything. Then in the meantime a little old smart-alecky Coast Guard outfit came around there and he was going to go in and get these men off, and he ran aground and ran inboard of this Victory—this was a Victory, not a Liberty—where he'd be in the calm and then he'd run high and dry on the same rocks and his ship was a total loss.

Q: Was it a cutter?

Chief Badders: No, it was a little old vessel of some kind that the Coast Guard had taken over from some company—a little old steam-driven thing, a little bigger than a seagoing tug, with about 35 men aboard in the crew. A young lieutenant (j.g.) was the commanding officer. That thing rolled right over on its side. But they came ashore. They got off of there. They launched life rafts and came ashore in life rafts. Then, besides the Victory ship, we have him and it's a total loss.

I had some of my most interesting experiences in the canal after the war. By the time the war was over, I had my men---the ones that were really interested in staying there---were by this time becoming exceptionally good divers and salvage men.

Q: How many did you have at that point?

Chief Badders: When the war was over, I had about 15, and that was adequate for the peacetime operation. About 15 divers, and I guess that's what they're trying to keep on hand now.

Q: But not really adequate for wartime?

Chief Badders: Not war, no. Fortunately we didn't have any big major accident during the war. I mean we didn't have a ship come in there loaded with explosives and blow up and plug the canal, and nobody knocked a gate out of one of the locks or anything of that kind that would have really caused 24 hours a day diving, day after day, until the job was completed. I wouldn't have had enough divers for that big a job.

Q: Does this say something about the effectiveness of security control?

Chief Badders: Right.

Q: Tell me about that.

Chief Badders: The thing about that, we were set up with a tie-in with the Navy that if we had a real disaster, of course the Navy would move right in and help us, bring their equipment and personnel, which was a relief. But the Navy, wonderful men, know all about salvage and diving and all that, but they didn't know all the answers in the Panama Canal like the men would have that I would have trained right on the scene. So it remained preferable to have had enough men of my own, trained there, local men, trained on the job to do the job that we anticipated might happen, but it never did, not big.

Q: Would you talk a little about the security measures which the authorities took during wartime to protect the canal from sabotage?

Chief Badders: One thing, every ship that went through the canal a crew of military people went aboard. Two Marines on the bridge and two machinist's mates in the engine room. One Marine on the bridge, when the pilot would ask for a signal to the engine room for a change of speed, handled the annunciator--the Marine handled the annunciator, the other Marine would write the bells down in a book. And the machinist's mates down in the engine room would see that those bells were answered properly and at the right time.

As I said before, we had had occasions when the pilot would ask for 10 degrees right rudder and he'd get 20 degrees left rudder. He'd ask for full ahead and get two-thirds astern or something. So with these people aboard that couldn't happen.

Then they had other men aboard--just how many I don't know, but they had a few Marines and a few Navy people aboard every ship that went through the canal. They would board at the pilothouse. They put a huge big barge, really a boathouse, before the entrances to the canal, and the pilots and these crews would be on these barges when the ships came by. And when the pilot went aboard, the designated number of men--military people--would go aboard, too. The number of military people varied according to the size of the ship and in some cases what the ship was loaded with. Lots of ammunition ships went through there, of course.

Q: And the military people would inspect the ship?

Chief Badders: Right. They would watch everything as closely as they could and, as I said, fortunately we really didn't have anything, any big sabotage, happen.

Q: Was neutral shipping barred from the use of the canal during the war?

Chief Badders: No, neutral shipping went through. All of our allies' shipping went through. We had no problems with any of them. They did some experimenting with a net thing—they called it the "billion-dollar folly." They devised a net, a big steel net, and when a ship went into a lock chamber, this net, which was on floats, came up under the ship, and if anything fell from the ship this net would catch it, and bells would ring, lights would flash, and all that kind of thing, and they'd rush this net out . . .

Q: And recover the loot!

Chief Badders: . . . Recover the loot. A beer can or anything else would set off the alarm. It didn't work out. It was abandoned. It looked beautiful on paper, but it was cumbersome and hard to handle, held up the ships. That didn't work. That was done away with.

Q: What about the question of fees, which are charged ordinarily in peacetime? In wartime what happened?

Chief Badders: I don't know. That is a phase of the Panama Canal that I never got the least bit interested in. I do know that fees today are almost the same as they were even before World War II, way before World War II. They haven't changed the fee rate in years and years in the canal. And it should have been increased a long time ago, but the shipping lobbyists are just too strong. Every time it comes up for a vote to increase the toll, as we called it down there, why, the shipping lobbyists would go to work and stop it.

Q: During wartime was there any real danger of sabotage from the local populace, or from agents working among the local people?

Chief Badders: It was known that there were agents in the area. In fact some were arrested. That was another part of my work down there. I was kind of assistant intelligence man to keep my eye on people and things, but they were never able to penetrate the defense and do anything down there that we knew of--at least, not that I knew of and I think I would have known if anything happened. They had cases of radio operators. They raided one place and found a complete radio installation where a man was relaying the information on the ships coming through the canal, what was aboard, and what ship size, even the name of the ship. They stopped that. A few things of that kind, but they never got around to where they could plant a charge anywhere and blow up anything.

Q: How well guarded was the canal?

Chief Badders: It was guarded as well as it could be. They had all kinds of military defenses around the canal. They had barrage balloons at all the lock areas, and searchlights, radio, all that business, and, of course, antiaircraft guns. We were a long time getting this stuff. The war had been going on quite a while before we had any antiaircraft guns down there. They figured it was important in other places, I guess, before we got it. They had thousands of military people and we had our air stations there, the submarine patrol, and all that business was operating all the time.

Q: Did they ultimately have radar also?

Chief Badders: Oh, yes, they had radar stations for spotting. It's a pretty complex place to defend really. Of course, now things on the site of the Panama Canal are practically useless. That's why they're pulling a lot of the military people out of there. They figure they've got to be 1,000 miles away to do any good protecting the canal now with bombs and stuff and missiles they can fly in.

One big worry with the canal was—you know Gatun Lake is held in place with a dam, and without Gatun Lake there is no Panama Canal. And that dam has a spillway in it for spilling the excess water, and there was always a fear that something might knock part of that spillway up and spill the water out of the Gatun Lake, and that would close the canal up until the spillway was repaired and the lake built up again. They built an underwater dam--well, I guess you could call it a dam; they called it a spillway. In other words, where this spillway was, there are 14 gates in the spillway that can be opened. Well, they built another spillway in front of that, all underwater, and bombproofed it. That was another diving job that we did there, and that was one of the jobs that held my diving school up because I was used on that job until it was completed.

The point of this thing was if they knocked the old spillway out--all the gates and everything were above water--this underwater spillway could be closed up by dropping gates in the steel structure that we left there and still hold the majority of the water in the Gatun Lake.

Q: It was a supplementary dam there?

Chief Badders: Right. But fortunately, there again, we never had to use the thing, but it was there if anything had happened. And many things could have happened. We had several alarms. People said one time that there was a raft of dynamite floating toward Gatun spillway. Of course, they had a power plant at this spillway, and it created a little current running in that direction all the time. Someone said they'd seen a raft floating toward the spillway and it'd be over there in another half-hour or so and blow that thing up. Well, that alerted everybody, all the lights and boats, but no raft was ever found.

Q: What was the attitude of the Panamanian Government and authorities at that time? Did they put any obstacles in the way of the operations, the smooth working of the canal?

Chief Badders: No, no. During the war they were very cooperative, as far as I know. I never heard of anything of any magnitude. Of course, by this time they were beginning to get money-hungry and seeing where they can get rich quick. They cut in on everything they could money-wise, but they didn't hamper the canal operation in any way. There was no way they could really. They couldn't even furnish the people we needed for laborers on the canal. We recruited people by the thousands from Colombia, Costa Rica, even some from Puerto Rico, but most of them were from Colombia, Venezuela, and all around that area. They worked on these new construction jobs and extra men in the shipyards.

We had a very busy shipyard situation there. Ships coming in there to go on to the Pacific or coming the other way going back to the Atlantic Force, by the time they'd hit there they'd need repair work of different kinds. We had a big bottom-cleaning program in the Balboa shop area. Big tankers would come in there if they'd been to sea long enough and were fouled up on the bottom and, of course, foul bottoms slow you down and require more power. They worked out a program where some of them stopped off there to get their bottoms cleaned. That required a lot of men because this had to be done quickly. That's when they first started using hot plastic paint on ships' bottoms, down there at least.

Q: Protects them from the barnacles.

Chief Badders: Right, take the barnacles and the sea growth off.

Q: I suppose there were examples of ships that were damaged by submarine activities in the Caribbean and thereabouts that had to come in there for emergency repairs?

Chief Badders: Right. We had one tanker—you could see it from the breakwater—that was torpedoed by a German submarine right close to our area, and he hit it on one side and knocked a tremendous hole in it. The ship rolled over on its side and the crew abandoned ship. The submarine surfaced to periscope depth and saw that he hadn't sunk the ship. Then he went around to the other side and fired another torpedo which hit right opposite where the first one hit, knocked a big hole in that side, and the ship rolled over back on an even keel and sat there, didn't sink. By this time we've got our patrol planes out, dropping depth charges and things, and the submarine took off.

Then, after they'd watched the thing for quite a while and seen that she wasn't going to sink, the crew went back aboard and brought it in closer to the breakwater. I took divers out and when they saw how much damage was done, it was safe to bring the ship through the canal. The first diver that went down and came back up said, "My God, the only thing holding that ship together, the two ends of it, is tank tops and the deck. If it didn't have a mast on it, you could drive a destroyer right through the ship." So I made my report and said that ship was liable to break in two at any minute.

There it's sitting and they looked at it---all this damage was below water---and it's sitting there looking pretty good. It had sunk some in the water, I think the draft had increased about 10 feet or something like that, which is nothing in a tanker. They determined they were going to take her through the canal to the Balboa dry dock. The dry dock in Cristobal wasn't large enough to take it. They took it over and put her in and they had lots of tugs and handled it very carefully, and when they pumped the water down and saw how much damage really was done to it, the port captain in Cristobal who had ordered this operation to proceed almost fainted. He said, "If I'd realized that ship was that nearly broken in two, it would never have gone through the Panama Canal."

We had another one come in there, and he was supposed to wait in an area for a pilot, but he didn't wait; he kept creeping on in. He got out of the channel and of course outside of this place was mined and he got over in the minefield. These mines were, some of them, contact mines and some of them could be exploded with a paddle over at Fort Sherman, and this mine officer sitting there watching this ship, going over in the minefield, and he sent a recognition signal to him and this fellow didn't answer anything. He didn't know any recognition signals---he was a Czechoslovakian, I believe. So the only thing for the mine officer to do was push the button on a mine right under him and blow him right out of the water. It raised his stern up and gave him a start, and he slid right straight across the channel with his stern sticking out about 50 feet right into the channel coming into Cristobal. He had a deckload of antiaircraft guns. We had to go out and get the antiaircraft guns and then with explosives get rid of the stern of that thing just sticking out in out channel.

Q: Those minefields were to prevent the submarines?

Chief Badders: Yes, or anything else.

By the way, we lost one of our submarines down there on the Pacific side, going out on patrol duty at night. The channel going through the minefield on the Pacific side was changed every so often and only a few people would know this channel where it would run through. Things had to be escorted through there. We had some cutters and things, and we had a great big yacht that the Navy had taken over and it was a so-called escort vessel, and that was its duty to escort people through the minefield. The commanding officer of this cutter would be informed of the route through the minefield.

Well, he had escorted these three S-type submarines through the minefield and when they get through the field, then he would cut off and come back in and they would go ahead. Of course, everything was blackened out. And when he cut off either he or the submarine, it was never determined, made a mistake and he rammed the sub and sank it, one of our submarines in about 320 feet of water.* I guess two or three men survived.

Q: Was there any danger from German raiders?

Chief Badders: They thought there was. They were prepared for that. You mean air or water?

---

*On the night of 24 January 1942, the USS S-26 (SS-131) was rammed by the PC-460 and sank in the Gulf of Panama. Of the crew, 46 men were lost and three survived.

Q: Water, raider ships.

Chief Badders: Well, no, they were more concerned with submarines than anything else. The submarines must have come in there awfully close, because we had a ship coming through the channel, right at the entrance to the breakwater, and it got something in its propeller and stopped the engines right there, just like it had hit a solid rock. Well, it drifted on in and they got tugs round it and brought it in to the dock, and sent for divers to go down and see what had happened to that propeller. I didn't have any diver available right at the time on the Atlantic side and this was a big hurry-up thing, so I got in gear and jumped down myself. When I got down there, it looked to me like a big hot-water tank or something had been picked up. It was a tank about 30 inches in diameter and about 6 or 8 feet long, and this thing had got crossways on the skeg, and the blade had hit it and just wrinkled it up around the tip of the blade, and the blade was right up and down over the skeg, and that's when it stopped.

I looked this thing over really well, and I looked up on one end of it and here's a round brass plate on it that had some kind of foreign language on it that I couldn't read. So I got out of there and came back up, and I sent for the mine officer or one of the mine officers over at Fort Sherman. By this time I suspected it might be a mine. I explained this whole thing to him, and he asked me to go down again, and take a better look at that plate and make out this lettering and bring it back to him, which I did. He said, "Well, it's a German mine," and he explained the type and everything else. Well, why didn't it go off, or what are we going to do to it from going off?

He said, "Well, that handhold plate that you see that had about 20 brass flat-head screws in it. Take them out and then you can pull that plate out and that will pull the detonator out. But you'll have to be careful when you do it."

So, when that operation got set up--we're not going to do that operation alongside the dock--the crew left the ship. They towed the ship out in the explosive area, and I took one tender with me and went down and took the screws out of this plate and started to bring it up.

Q: You did that job yourself?

Chief Badders: Yes. I moved the thing about 6 inches, and it wouldn't come any farther, got jammed. Well, I'm not going to force it--he told me not to put any force on it and be careful it doesn't hit the sides when it comes out--he explained it to me it was a thing about so long.

Well, I came back out and explained all this to him. I'd get him to come out and backed the boat away from this thing a couple of hundred yards before he can come out. I talked to him and he said, "Well, that detonator is down in there so far that that kink in the housing of the mine has got it jammed and you can't get it out."

This was an ammunition ship loaded with ammunition. Well, they want to get this out, they want to get the ammunition to its destination. They didn't want to unload it and transfer it to another ship. That would take days and days to do that down there. So I said I'd try one thing. I took a big long section of another chain and took a loop around that blade that was over the tank, the mine---by this time we're calling it a mine; we're not calling it a tank any longer. And I got one of our biggest tugs there and put two tow wires, his tow wire and another one, which put him a couple of thousand yards away from the ship, hooked up to the chain and he was right abeam of this thing. I made him back up to where he had a lot of slack in the wire and then go ahead just as hard as he could go, full speed, and jerk that blade to see if he couldn't jerk it back the way it went in. And, sure enough, it came clear, and it didn't explode.

Of course, I'm back out of the way of that operation when that happened; there was nothing near the ship.

Q: You'd think the jolt would have . . .

Chief Badders: The blade wasn't damaged enough to prevent the ship from going ahead, so it was only held up about a day with a

German mine it picked up right in the entrance of the Cristobal breakwater. Whether that thing had been somewhere and floated in there, or whether it had been planted somewhere close to that area or dropped off . . .

Q: Was that area swept with great regularity?

Chief Badders: Oh, yes, we had torpedo nets out there all the time, harbor nets, you know, and they had to be opened for every ship that went through and closed all the time, and boats ran back and forth with sounding equipment. But they didn't go outside the breakwater very often. I think they did after that. I think they began patroling father out at sea.

I had heard reports of Navy planes spotting submarines out there, outside our minefields, and dropped depth charges down to run them off. There was no record of any of them ever being sunk or captured out there, but they did claim sightings.

Q: What about the other side, the Balboa side?

Chief Badders: We never had any problems over there.

Q: Wasn't there always the fear that the Japs might come along?

Chief Badders: Well, we were standing around there with our hair standing straight up on our heads after Pearl Harbor. We just couldn't understand why they didn't come on and do the same thing to the Panama Canal. Then, of course, we found out later that they didn't want to damage the canal; they wanted to use it themselves. That was the only reason they didn't. There wasn't a thing in the world to keep them from coming on and just blowing the Panama Canal right out of existence.

Q: I didn't know that story, that they wanted to use it.

Chief Badders: Sure, they didn't want to damage the canal, or they could have come ahead from Pearl Harbor. We didn't have enough Navy left then to stop them. We didn't know what was going to happen around there for a while, after Pearl Harbor.

Q: At one time there were some vague ideas that we might do something about fortifying the Galapagos and islands in that area.

Chief Badders: Yes, we had a lot of people out there. I went out there twice working on underwater pipelines and cables. It was sounding stuff, radar signal relay, and that kind of stuff. There wasn't much of a defense out there, but there were quite a few military people on that barren rock. What a place to do duty! Miles and miles from nowhere.

Q: Those must have been exciting days for you and strenuous ones, as you say.

Chief Badders: Yes, the days just weren't long enough, and there weren't enough of them to keep up with things that were going on; that was the trouble. I worked myself right down to a nub.

Q: You didn't have much family life?

Chief Badders: Very little. My wife would see me sometimes like today and I'd go off on jobs and when I went on a job I just had to stay until the job was finished. A lot of times I'd work as many as four days and nights without ever stopping. Then there were many jobs where I'd be out a week or two on the job. Of course, there would be rest periods at that time. But I've been on jobs that were in such a stage that I just didn't even stop.

That was one of the problems with my job down there. I should have had another man at least in my capacity, somebody who could relieve me.

I was on one job, and this was after the war, too. I'd been on the job four days and five nights, brought the ship back into the dock in the explosive area in the morning and my boss by this time is the marine superintendent, a Navy captain. He saw me and said, "When were you home last?" I had on a pair of khaki shorts and an old what had been white sweatshirt and a golf cap and a pair of sneakers. I was filthy dirty and I guess my eyes must have looked like burnt holes in a blanket.

I said, "I haven't been home since we took the ship out to the explosive area." I'd lost all track of time. After you've been up a certain length of time, you don't get sleepy anymore. You lose track of everything.

Q: But you're not quite as sharp as you were!

Chief Badders: That's the point, exactly. You can hurt yourself or hurt somebody else by not being as alert as you should be. Well, he sent me home, and right then was the crucial point of this operation. The ship had been on fire alongside the dock. They thought they had the fire out—they did have the fire out—a chemist and other people were going through the ship looking for gas and explosive areas before they could let people do different types of work, and they were down in the refrigerating section of the ship and went into the refrigerator part of the cold storage. There was no gas in there, but they opened a door to go into the freezer section of the refrigerator compartment, and somebody must have struck a match right at that time or was smoking a cigarette or something, and that thing was full of explosive gas and it blew up and killed three men and maimed four or five others—a big thing about it.

So immediately this ship was grabbed and rushed out of there, taken to the explosive area, and that's when I went aboard. It had a lot of soybeans aboard, and we found out right then—it may have been known before, but I didn't know it and no one I talked to down there did—soybeans soaked in salt water put out 100% explosive gas. These soybeans were swelling up like popcorn. A soybean is not too big, but when that thing is soaked in salt water it's six to eight times its normal size. Several of the cargo holds of this ship were full of these bulk soybeans, and they were swelling up and throwing off this gas. I had to get rid of the beans.

Q: Did you get a special citation for all of this tremendous work?

Chief Badders: No, I have a folder full of letters of commendation. It was my job. That was what I was hired for.

I say "I" had to get rid of these beans, but I must have had 15 or 20 men working with me on that job. We moved those things with airlifts. They wouldn't let us use any kind of metallic equipment like shovels. Normally, to unload something like that you bring a crane alongside with a big scoop . . .

Q: Why? Because of the friction?

Chief Badders: Yes, they're afraid that a clamshell might hit a hatch railing or something and make a spark and blow this thing up. We opened one of the hatch covers and this water would start working on these beans, and they'd swell up and run out over that hatch foaming just like popping popcorn. The darnedest thing I ever saw. I pumped I don't know how many hundred tons of soybeans right over the side in the Pacific.

After this operation had been going on for a couple of days, then the wildlife people got interested: "What's this going to do to the fish?" That's the greatest fishing country in the world down there. We found out that the fish just got good and fat on it. They loved it. When we first dumped some of these over, they would sink to the bottom and then a day or two later they'd all come back up to the surface again. They were lying on the water out there it looked for miles, like an oil slick really.

Q: Did they discover any use for this gas produced by soybeans?

Chief Badders: No. Actually, I don't believe the gas was as bad as they said it was. I don't believe it was that gas that blew up. In fact, I know it wasn't that gas that blew up in this freezer compartment, because there was no way for it to get in there. I think the gas in there--well, I don't have any idea what kind of gas it was and nobody else did find out, because when it exploded the gas all deteriorated and there was no way of getting a sample of it. A couple of my good friends were hurt badly on that job. The chemist was killed.

In navy yard routine, when a ship is damaged, any work is going on on the ship that's in closed compartments or compartments that have been closed, and particularly a damaged ship, the chemist has to completely analyze the ship for gases and all that stuff. The chemist should have just been doubly sure that the people behind him were not smoking or getting ready to smoke or anything. Evidently he hadn't checked as well as he should. Of course, it's possible that something else could have set this off when he opened the door, but they couldn't think of anything else that would do it. Two or three men who survived in this work party said they thought they had seen a match struck or a cigarette lighter lit just before the explosion. They couldn't be positive.

But we had to unload this ship out in this explosive area. Then the operation of going around and trying to detect where this gas came from. You could smell this gas coming from the beans. They took a sample of that, and the chemist got all excited. The report was that it was 100% explosive, and it had to be unloaded before the ship could come back alongside the dock---that is, all the beans that were wet or liable to get wet.

That was the operation I worked on so long without stopping, because we were way out and it took a long time to get set up and get in and out, so I just stayed there.

I made a lot of trips from the Panama Canal to other

countries down there. The canal would loan me to other countries for jobs. I went to Nicaragua and did a job for old President Somoza, the one who was assassinated, not the young son who's dictator down there now, but the original old Somoza that the United States put in power when there was trouble in Nicaragua.*

We had a yacht on that lake down there, Lake Managua, and another tugboat. They were the only two vessels in the lake and they came together and sunk his yacht, and he wanted his yacht raised.

Q: This was during the war?

Chief Badders: Right after. I worked with him for about six weeks, I guess I was down there, to raise his yacht.

Q: Did they treat you well while you were down there?

Chief Badders: Very well. I thought I was eating like a king. We lived right on this other tugboat that had sunk his yacht. We were working from that, and a big banana barge, and he was living right there on the job. All the food that came aboard, anything like fish, any fowl, even pigs, were brought aboard alive. All

---

*Anastasio Somoza (1896-1956), president of Nicaragua from 1937 to 1947. His son, General Anastasio Somoza Debayle (1925-1980) was president from 1967 until his overthrow by Sandinista rebels in 1979).

water came aboard in locked cans, drinking water. Milk was in locked cans. The food was, I thought, out of this world, and it was. But one day I happened to be down below around the galley and I saw one of the cooks come out---this tugboat had only about 2 feet of freeboard, he could reach over the side and dip water out of the lake in this bucket, and this was right aft of one of the head discharges where the water was running right aft on the ship and he must have got some of that discharge into his bucket. I watched what he was going to do with it and he went in the galley and dumped it in the sink and that's what he was washing dishes in! Well, right then I got sick. I couldn't eat anything on that ship anymore, and I had about two weeks to go yet! I had all kinds of stomach problems from then on. The only thing I ate was bread and stuff like that, jelly, cheese, goat cheese. I ate goat cheese three times a day, and guava jelly. I just about lived on that the last two or three weeks I was there.

When we got ready to leave, he gave us all a present. I had a Navy commander with me who was kind of a liaison officer. The Navy really engineered this deal. It was one of those lend-lease things, you know, us and the equipment, and we took this Navy commander along as a liaison man between him, me, and the commandant of the 15th Naval District. By this time, we'd gotten really well acquainted with old man Somoza---he was a character---and he said, "I'm going to give the commander a medal. I can't decorate you fellows. [I had two divers with me and a couple or three colored fellows as diver tenders.] I can't give you fellows medals, you're civilians, so I'll have my aide decorate you when we get into Managua." And he gave each of us a dozen handkerchiefs, myself and my two divers, that he said he had specially handmade. I believe my wife must still have them around here—the most beautiful things you've ever seen—handmade lace handkerchiefs.

We didn't know how we were going to be decorated when we got into Managua, but we were going to have to lay there for a day or two before a plane came in to take us back to Panama.

Q: That's a dull place!

Chief Badders: Yes. We went in by train and when we got there a Nicaraguan Army captain—I guess he was Army—met us and took us to the hotel and he told the hotel manager when we went in to register that everything we wanted—it didn't make any difference what it was we ordered—went on the bill to be sent to the President. Then he handed each one of us an envelope and said, "This is from the President," and in the envelope were three $100 bills, brand-new $100 bills. That was our decoration!

He was quite a man. I talked with him a lot on that job, and I got to really like him. You know, he was considered to be a dictator in that country, making millions off of the country and off of the people, but he told me and I believe he was right, that he only did things for the good of his country, and he had built schools, he'd built roads, he'd built hospitals. He said, "I go up here in the mountains and I find a stand of mahogany [and they had beautiful mahogany in Nicaragua.] I try to get people interested in going up there to get that mahogany out of there and sell it, make money for the country and for themselves, too. Nobody's interested. They won't do it. So I go do it. I put men up there. I might use some of my road equipment trucks to haul it out and things of that kind, but I'm putting men to work. I'm making money and there's money going in the treasury."

I really think they assassinated the wrong man when they shot him. That son of his who took over when he left, he was a stinker. He was a West Point graduate, too, his son.*

Q: Was he? He's not so much for the people as for himself.

Chief Badders: No. He's arrogant, overbearing. At the time this happened, our commercial air terminal was in the Canal Zone, they flew out of Albrook Field---they hadn't built the big Tocumen Airport out in Panama yet---and he'd been in Panama for something and he had to go down to the airport to catch a plane and go back to Nicaragua. And he came in the lobby of that terminal with double holsters and a big pearl-handled revolver in each

---

*General Somoza graduated in the West Point class of 1946.

holster--in the Canal Zone to catch a plane to go to Nicaragua. They had a big hassle over that, trying to get him to get rid of the guns. This was shortly after he had relieved his father.

When the old man was shot, they brought him to the Canal Zone. He was in the Canal Zone hospital when he died. He always wore a scarf round his neck and he had a ring that he'd slip up over the two ends of the scarf to hold it together up under his chin, and that thing must have had a ten-carat diamond in it. It looked like a headlight hanging under his chin. I told him one day, "You're going to lose that ring off that scarf. It's going to slip off and drop overboard or something, and you're going to lose it." But he was still wearing it when I left him.

We used to go to all those countries down there. All the oil companies had offshore oil lines where they didn't have piers to bring their tankers in and unload. The tankers would pick up the hose at the end of the pipeline and pump the oil ashore. They were invariably having trouble with them. They'd slip in their moorings and break their hoses, or their pipes would get holes in them, deteriorate, and send divers. In some cases I went with them.

I went to where they were building the transamerican highway, building a bridge across one of the rivers, and they had some caisson trouble. I helped them out with that.

Q: That must have been in Guatemala, wasn't it?

Chief Badders: No. It was San Jose, Costa Rica.

So, all in all, the Panama Canal job was really an interesting job. When the war was over, I figured that I didn't know what was going to happen. That was one thing that I was a little perturbed about, but they left me on inactive duty all during the war down there with civilian status. I went down there as a chief petty officer and had been since 1926. I was a senior master diver in the Navy and had had experience in salvaging three submarines, and I figured that I was the leading man in the enlisted ranks in that type of work. They must have figured that, too, or they wouldn't have sent me down there. They'd have sent me somewhere else.

Well, I felt that after the war hit and I'd look around and see all the shipmates of mine going up to lieutenant and lieutenant commander, commander, and whatnot, if I'd been on active duty I'd have had that same opportunity.

Q: Naturally!

Chief Badders: Which I didn't have on inactive duty. I couldn't get advanced.

Then when the war's over, here I am still a chief petty officer, civilian. Panama Canal have decided by this time that they want this installation of mine to be a permanent part of the Panama Canal for future protection of the canal, to assist shipping and all that. They told me that they were going to keep the diving school and everything as it was—cut down on some of the equipment and some of the personnel—but to keep a force for me to figure out what was required for a force for ship repairs and construction work that might come up in peacetime operations. And they said that they would like for me to stay on the job. So I told them I would stay if they would make it Civil Service which all the employment in the Panama Canal is, so I dated back to the time I went there in March of 1940, and they did.

Q: You had some sort of tenure?

Chief Badders: Right. When I finally retired from there, I had 23 years' service in the canal and 22-1/2 years in the Navy—45 years and some months' government service. But I would have loved to have had the opportunity at least to have a commission at some time. I'm sure I would have had it.

Q: Did you make any effort to do this after the war?

Chief Badders: Nothing could be done after the war. I wasn't the only one in that situation.

Q: Your high-placed friends in the Navy might have helped you.

Chief Badders: There were attempts to do it. McNamara, even, was interested at one time.* He said, "Well, it wasn't right. I don't see why we couldn't make a paper commission anyway." When I retired I combined my Navy service with my civil service. In other words, I take one paycheck instead of two. I would have taken a Navy check and a Civil Service check, or you can combine military with Civil Service and take one.

Q: That's more pleasing to the comptroller to make one!

Chief Badders: Not only that, but it increased my Civil Service time and gave me much more money than I would—not much more, but some. So if they were to give me a commission even now it would only be paper, it wouldn't be money-wise, but it would have given me the privileges and the social standing. Down there I was considered one of the big wheels, or whatever, in the canal and we went everywhere. We were accepted everyplace, in admirals' quarters, at admirals' parties, and the governor's parties, and everything else. But then every once in a while we'd be around some officers' club at a cocktail party or something—my wife never told me about this, but I know it happened—some officer's wife would ask her, "What's your husband's rank?" Well, she wouldn't think and tell them I was Civil Service; she'd say chief

---
*Robert S. McNamara, Secretary of Defense from 1961 to 1968.

petty officer. Frost kind of fell after that.

Q: It does with some people!

Chief Badders: Yes, but to the people that count it didn't make any difference.

Q: Were you tempted at all to live down there permanently?

Chief Badders: Well, you can't live there, except live in Panama and I wouldn't live in Panama--no, I wouldn't even have lived in the Canal Zone. We wanted to get out when we did. We had become kind of tired of the place. It's monotonous, and politics were getting rough. I think we left at a good time.

I would have worked for a few more years. I was healthy, felt good, and I could have done a good job for another four or five years, but to not be working, I wouldn't have stayed there, which I didn't. As soon as my time was up we got out of there. I worked as long as I could. You have to retire down there when you reach 62.

Q: That's considered foreign duty and you have to?

Chief Badders: Right. But it's a shame, because not only me but other people had to go out down there the same way who were perfectly capable of doing a good job for a few years longer, and a lot of them wanted to. I didn't ask to, but I don't believe they would have let me stay anyway.

That's one of the reasons we came to this part of the country to settle down. We got so darned tired of everything being green all year long and warm all year. We like the change of seasons, but I tell you these winters are getting colder for me every winter!

Q: Well, you've got a great career to contemplate, a really great career, and I thank you very much.

Index to

Series of Taped Interviews

with

Chief Machinist's Mate William Badders, USN (Ret.)

Asiatic Fleet
   Lack of master divers in early 1930s, pp. 44-45; athletics, pp. 59-65; personnel anxious to get off Asiatic Station, p. 66

Athletics
   At Great Lakes in 1919, p. 4; at Pensacola in early 1920s, pp. 4-5, 7; golf in Far East in 1930s, pp. 59, 61, 64; See: Football; Baseball; Crew Olympics

Athletics---Naval Academy
   Anecdotes about crew and coaches in the early 1920s, pp. 10-12; head football coach in the mid-1940s got coaching experience with submarine division team in mid-1930s, p. 69

Badders, Chief Machinist's Mate William, USN (Ret.)
   Awards and commendations, pp. 3, 26, 30, 49, 102-104; health, pp. 30, 65-66, 68; family, pp. 44, 106, 143, 155-156; enlists in 1918 and sent to Great Lakes, pp. 1-2; service in battleship Wisconsin (BB-9), 1918-1919, pp. 2-4; reports for duty at Great Lakes in 1919, p. 4; squadron maintenance work at Pensacola in early 1920s, pp. 4-7; engineer in battleship Kansas (BB-21), 1921, pp. 7-9; engineer in Reina Mercedes (IX-25) at Naval Academy, 1921-1924, pp. 10-13; joins engineering department of Falcon (ARS-2) and helps with S-51 (SS-162) rescue, 1924-1926, pp. 13-29; stationed in Reina Mercedes (IX-25) and plays semipro football, 1926-1927, pp. 29-30; returns to the Falcon (ARS-2), 1927-1928, pp. 30-36; student and instructor at new diving school at Naval Gun Factory, 1928-1930, pp. 36-37, 39-40; master diver in Falcon (ARS-2), 1930-1931, pp. 38-44; master diver in Pigeon (AM-47) in the early 1930s, pp. 44-66; master diver in Holland (AS-3) in the mid-1930s, pp. 66-71; joins experimental diving unit in Washington in late 1930s, pp. 71-73, 75-104; master diver-salvage master as civilian in the Panama Canal, 1940-1962, pp. 73-75, 98-99, 104-157

Balloons
   Free and observation balloons at Pensacola in the early 1920s, pp. 5-6

Barracudas
   Problem to Navy divers off Key West, pp. 51-52

Baseball
   Pensacola Air Station baseball team among first transported to games by air in early 1920s, p. 5; Badders plays on professional team in Manila in early 1930s, pp. 59, 61-64; Badders plays with submarine division team in China that wins

championship three years in a row, pp. 59-60, 65; popularity of game with naval personnel in Far East in 1930s, p. 60; quality of black league in 1930s, pp. 62-64; See: Gehrig, Lou; Paige, Leroy "Satchel"; Williams, Ted

Blimps
See: Lighter-than-air

Brooklyn Navy Yard
See: New York Navy Yard

Brumby, Rear Admiral Frank H., USN (USNA, 1895)
As Commander Submarine Divisions Control Force in late 1920s had to field outcry by media about S-4 (SS-108) crew members who were not able to be rescued, p. 34

City of Rome, MV
Rams S-51 (SS-162) off Block Island, New York, on 25 September 1925 and picks up survivors, pp. 18-19

Coal-burning Ships
Method of selecting enlisted personnel for during World War I, pp. 1-2; Badders fudges on form to get duty in engine room rather than fireroom, pp. 2-3

Coast Guard, U.S.
In charge of keeping boats out of the way when S-51 (SS-162) towed into New York Harbor in 1926, p. 25; cutter Paulding rams S-4 (SS-108) off Massachusetts in 1928, pp. 31-32; role in Squalus (SS-192) rescue in May 1939, p. 84; Coast Guard vessel attempts to rescue crew from victory ship grounded in Panama Canal during World War II and goes aground herself, pp. 125-126

Cole, Rear Admiral Cyrus W., USN (USNA, 1899)
As commandant of the Portsmouth Navy Yard in May 1939 and officer in charge of Squalus (SS-192) rescue, sends chamber down again after obvious survivors saved to ensure there are no others, pp. 87-88; Squalus finally able to be lifted from ocean floor on 21 June 1939, Admiral Cole's birthday, pp. 99-100

Commissioned Officers
Badders regrets that his inactive status during World War II prevented him from being commissioned, as many of his friends were, pp. 153-156

Crew
    U.S. Naval Academy crew that won 1920 Olympic gold medal brought back together in 1924 to try again, pp. 11-12; See: Glendon, Richard J.; Glendon, Richard J., Jr.

Disasters
    Free balloon lost at Pensacola in early 1920s, p. 6; F-boat sunk off Honolulu in 1914, pp. 28-29; Japanese ship grounds and turns over with some loss of life in early 1930s, pp. 49-50, 53-55; American S-type submarine accidentally rammed by pilot ship at Panama Canal in World War II, p. 137; vessel loaded with soybeans catches fire and explodes at Panama in the mid-1940s, pp. 143-147; See: S-51 (SS-162); S-4 (SS-108); Squalus (SS-192)

Diving
    Navy's program in the mid-1920s extremely weak, pp. 17, 21, 28-29, 34; hazard of cold weather diving, pp. 20-21; as part of S-51 (SS-162) salvage in 1925-1926, p. 22; push for more and better quality divers in 1926, p. 28; attempts to rescue crew members from S-4 (SS-108) in December 1927, p. 31; failure with S-4 brings about more money and interest in Navy's diving program, p. 34; pay bonuses for divers, p. 45; lack of master divers on Asiatic Station in 1930s, pp. 44-45; protocol for order of diving, p. 46; hazard of night diving in Far East, pp. 46-47; drills for rescuing submarine crews in early 1930s, pp. 38, 57; depths for diving qualifications, p. 58; helium and oxygen experimented with in late 1930s, pp. 76-81; developments in the early 1970s, pp. 91-95; dangers of deep depth diving, pp. 95-96; health factors, pp. 96-99; diver tenders, p. 112; Badders sent on odd diving jobs in Caribbean, pp. 152-153; See: Rescue Operations; Sharks; Barracudas; Humboldt Current; Experimental Diving Unit; Navy Diving School; Diving--Training

Diving--Training
    Poor quality of training in Washington, D.C., in mid-1920s, p. 17; difficulty keeping divers qualified on Asiatic Station in early 1930s, pp. 45, 57; in Panama Canal during World War II, pp. 108-116, 118; See: Navy Diving School

Eagle-class Patrol Boats
    Used with lighter-than-air planes at Pensacola in early 1920s, p. 5

Edison, Charles
    Secretary of the Navy Edison reenacts presenting Medal of Honor to Badders and three other Squalus (SS-192) rescuers in January 1940, pp. 103-104

Ellsberg, Lieutenant Commander Edward, USN (USNA, 1914)
   In charge of salvage work on S-51 (SS-162) in the mid-1920s, pp. 22-23; makes suggestions for improvements after S-51 salvage in 1926, p. 26; recommends Badders for promotion to chief in 1926, p. 30

Engineering Duty
   Badders's duties as new recruit in Wisconsin (BB-9) in 1918, p. 3; engineering crew does half of overhaul to USS Falcon (ARS-2) in 1924, pp. 13-14

England
   Poor quality of ships passing through Panama Canal during World War II, p. 121

Experimental Diving Unit
   Divers used as guinea pigs to establish standards, pp. 75-76; divers return from Squalus (SS-192) salvage to do paperwork, pp. 101-102

Falcon, USS (ARS-2)
   Poor condition when Badders reported aboard in 1924 during overhaul and turnaround by 1925, pp. 13-15; another overhaul in 1925, p. 16; sent to aid sunken S-51 (SS-162) in September 1925, pp. 16-26; cruise to Panama with subs in early 1926, p. 21; part of rescue and salvage effort of S-4 (SS-108) in late 1927-early 1928, pp. 30-34; conducts submarine rescue drills in early 1930s, pp. 38-39; helium/oxygen mixture for divers tested in cold weather dives, pp. 77, 80-81; aids in Squalus rescue in May 1939, pp. 83-89

Fireman Rating
   Method of choosing enlisted men during World War I, pp. 1-2

Football
   Pensacola Air Station football team among first to be transported to games by air in early 1920s, pp. 4-5; officers and enlisted men on team in early 1920s, p. 7; Badders plays with Reina Mercedes semipro team in mid-1920s, p. 29; Badders plays with submarine division team while in Holland (AS-3) in mid-1930s, pp. 68-70

Frazer, Chief Torpedoman James W., USN
   As one of the Navy's few divers in the 1920s, works on both S-51 and S-4, p. 33

Galapagos Islands
   Fortified during World War II, p. 142

Gehrig, Lou
    Brings American baseball players to Manila in the 1930s to play pro teams that included many American military personnel and businessmen, p. 62

Glendon, Richard J.
    Coach of 1920 Naval Academy Olympic gold medal-winning crew team brought out of retirement in 1924 to try again, p. 12

Glendon, Richard J., Jr.
    Anecdote concerning 1920s Naval Academy crew coach, pp. 10-11

Good, Lieutenant Roscoe F., USN (USNA, 1920)
    Coaches submarine division baseball team in China to championship three years in a row in the 1930s, pp. 59-60, 65

Great Lakes, Illinois
    Boot training during World War II, pp. 1-2; athletics in 1919, p. 4

Hagberg, Lieutenant (j.g.) Oscar E., USN (USNA, 1931)
    Coaches successful submarine division football team at San Diego in mid-1930s, p. 69

Hartley, Lieutenant Henry, USN
    Encourages Badders to become involved in salvage duty in mid-1920s, p. 13; shapes up _Falcon_ (ARS-2) upon reporting as commanding officer in 1924, p. 14; proponent of expanding rescue and salvage capabilities in mid-1920s, pp. 17, 28; makes recommendations for improvements after _S-51_ salvage in 1926, p. 26; sets up diving school in Washington, D.C., in 1928, pp. 35-37

Holland, USS (AS-3)
    Equipped to lift ships from her bow, p. 67; baseball team in the mid-1930s, p. 68

Hollowell, Lieutenant Commander John A., Jr., USN (USNA, 1922)
    As head of the experimental diving unit at Washington, D.C., in mid-1930s, requests Badders join unit, pp. 70-71

Humboldt Current
    Badders plunges into cold current while conducting experimental dives from _Mallard_ (ASR-4) in late 1930s, pp. 78-79

Japan
  Passenger ship grounds and turns over with some loss of life in early 1930s, pp. 49-50, 53-55; Panama Canal not attacked in World War II because Japanese wanted to use it themselves, pp. 141-142; See: Kaku Maru

Kaku Maru
  Pigeon (AM-374) goes to rescue of this Japanese merchant vessel, on fire in the China Sea in the early 1930s, and discovers later that she was hiding aviation fuel, pp. 48-49, 55-56

Kansas, USS (BB-21)
  Badders assigned as engineer for admiral's barge in 1921, p. 7; crew plays non-stop baseball for Norwegians during summer cruise in 1921, p. 89; decommissioned in December 1921, p. 9

King, Captain Ernest J., USN (USNA, 1901)
  As commander of the New London submarine base during 1926 S-51 (SS-162) salvage operation, tells Badders to wear heavy buoyant life jacket during dangerous maneuver that hinders his effort, p. 24; Badders flies with King from Annapolis to Boston to aid in rescue effort on S-4 (SS-108) in December 1927, p. 31; advises Badders to get into aviation in the late 1920s and later disapproves his request to do so, pp. 34-35

Lafayette, USS (AP-53)
  Salvage of this French liner at New York pier diverts Badders and equipment from Panama Canal, pp. 109-110

Liberty Ship
  Poor quality of construction poses problems during World War II transits of Panama Canal, p. 21

Lighter-than-air
  Aircraft at Pensacola in early 1920s, p. 5

Mallard, USS (ASR-4)
  Badders chilled by Humboldt current during experimental dives from this ship in late 1930s, pp. 78-79

Marine Corps, U.S.
  Football team at San Diego in mid-1930s, pp. 69-70; Marines boarded all ships during World War II Panama Canal transits, pp. 127-128

Mariveles Bay
  Badders has close call with coral snakes during night dive in early 1930s, pp. 46-47

McCann Chamber
   Selected for further experimentation by divers in the 1930s, pp. 40, 43; used in Squalus (SS-192) rescue in May 1939, pp. 84-87

McNamara, Robert S.
   As Secretary of Defense, interested in obtaining commission for Badders in early 1960s, p. 155

Medal of Honor
   Badders and three others receive this award for 1939 Squalus (SS-192) rescue in January 1940, pp. 102-104

Michels, Chief Torpedoman James W., USN
   Sent from Newport Torpedo Station to aid in S-51 (SS-162) salvage effort in 1925-1926, p. 18; life endangered during S-4 rescue attempt in December 1927, p. 32

Mihalowski, Torpedoman First Class John, USN
   Role in Squalus (SS-192) rescue in May 1939, pp. 85, 103

Mines
   Czechoslavakian ship blown up in Panama Canal during World War II, p. 136; ship transitting Panama Canal fouls propeller on German mine, pp. 138-141

Momsen, Lieutenant Commander Charles B., USN (USNA, 1920)
   As head of Navy experimental diving unit in May 1939, oversees Squalus (SS-192) rescue, pp. 82, 87; See: Momsen Lung

Momsen Lung
   Experimented with in the early 1930s and all submariners trained in its use, pp. 40-43

Morale
   Haphazard conditions during overhaul of Falcon (ARS-2) in 1924 improved with new commanding officer, pp. 13-15

Naval Academy, U.S.
   Midshipman cruise in Kansas (BB-21) in 1921, pp. 8-9

Naval Gun Factory, Washington, D.C.
   Navy diving school established in 1928, pp. 35-37

Navy Diving School
   Established at Naval Gun Factory in late 1920s, pp. 35-36; class sizes, p. 36; training, pp. 39-40

NC-4
   Lieutenant Commander Albert C. Read, USN, visits Pensacola in NC-4 in early 1920s, pp. 6-7

Newport, Rhode Island
   Site of Navy's diving program in mid-1920s, p. 17

New York Navy Yard
   Workmen race to bring Falcon (ARS-2) out of overhaul to rescue S-51 (SS-162) in September 1925, p. 16; S-51 (SS-162) brought to yard after being raised in 1926, p. 25; See: Plunkett, Rear Admiral Charles P., USN

Nicaragua
   See: Somoza, Anastasio; Somoza Debayle, General Anastasio

Normande, SS
   See: Lafayette, USS (AP-53)

Norway
   USS Kansas (BB-21) crew entertains Norwegians in Christiania (Oslo) with non-stop baseball in summer of 1921, pp. 8-9

Olympics
   1920 gold medal winning crew from U.S. Naval Academy sets out to duplicate feat in 1924, but is thwarted by Yale, pp. 11-12

Ortolan, USS (ASR-5)
   Holland (AS-3) divers made re-qualifying dives from this ship in mid-1930s, p. 68

Paige, Leroy "Satchel"
   Badders gets hit of a lifetime off of pitcher Paige when the black baseball star brought an American team to play in Manila, pp. 62-63

Panama Canal
   Underwater welding equipment and techniques employed during World War II, pp. 73-75; warm water diving experiments conducted here in late 1930s, pp. 78-79; Badders leaves active duty to take job as master diver-salvage master in 1940, pp. 104-106; living situation, pp. 106, 156; backward nature of diving before Badders's arrival, p. 107; Badders initiates plans to keep canal functioning during wartime that includes diving school, pp. 108-116, 118-119, 133-136; assessment of Panamanians, pp. 113-114, 133; dual role of divers, pp. 114-115; pipelines, p. 116; grounded ships, pp. 117-118, 121-126; ship sizes and numbers passing through canal during World War

II, pp. 119-120; post-war diving contingent, pp. 126, 153-154; security during war, pp. 127-131, 141; importance of Lake Gatun, pp. 131-133; mines, pp. 136-141; Japanese didn't attack canal because they wanted it for themselves, pp. 141-142; round-the-clock work on a burning ship full of soybeans, pp. 143-147; Badders's World War II setup made permanent after the war, pp. 153-154

Parachutes
Available but not used at Pensacola in early 1920s, p. 6

Paulding, USCGC
Rams S-4 (SS-108) off Provincetown, Massachusetts, in December 1927, pp. 31-32

Pensacola
Athletics in early 1920s, pp. 4-5, 7; aircraft at Pensacola in early 1920s discussed, pp. 5-6

Philippine Islands
Badders plays on pro baseball team in 1930s, pp. 59, 61-64; golf a popular pasttime for naval personnel in 1930s, pp. 61, 64

Piccard, Auguste
French diver's role in development of pressurized diving vessels in 1940s, pp. 94-95

Pigeon, USS (AM-47)
Operating schedule in Asiatic Fleet in early 1930s, pp. 44-45; puts out fire on Japanese merchant ship and learns later that she was hiding aviation fuel, pp. 48-49, 55-56; rescues passengers from a Japanese ship that runs aground in early 1930s, pp. 49-50, 53-55; practices sub rescues, p. 57; anecdote showing ship commanding officer and Badders's desire to get off Asiatic Station, pp. 65-66

Plunkett, Rear Admiral Charles P., USN (USNA, 1884)
As commandant of the Brooklyn Navy Yard in September 1925 orders the Falcon (ARS-2), temporarily laid up for a minor overhaul, to make immediate repairs and go to the aid of the sunken S-51 (SS-162), p. 16; selects Lieutenant Commander Ellsberg to head S-51 salvage effort, pp. 19-20

Promotion
Procedure for making chief in mid-1920s, p. 30

Read, Lieutenant Commander Albert C., USN (USNA, 1907)
Visits Pensacola in NC-4 after his historic 1919 transatlantic flight, pp. 6-7

Reina Mercedes, USS (IX-25)
   Location at the Naval Academy in 1921, p. 10; officers aboard in 1921, pp. 12-13; Badders member of this ship's semipro football team in mid-1920s, pp. 29-30

Rescue Operations
   Divers from Newport sent to sunken S-51 (SS-162) in September 1925 determined that no one was alive, p. 18; officers make suggestions for changes aboard submarines after S-51 (SS-162) salvage, p. 26; attempts to save crew members from S-4 (SS-108) in December 1927 futile, pp. 31-33; drills with submarines in early 1930s, pp. 38, 57; method of escape from a submarine in 1930s, p. 41; victory ship ran aground during World War II in Panama Canal, pp. 121-125; See: McCann Chamber; Momsen Lung

Royal Navy
   Status of salvage operation in Hong Kong in early 1930s, p. 51

S-4, USS (SS-108)
   Rammed by Coast Guard cutter Paulding in December 1927, pp. 31-32; futile attempt to rescue six crew members, pp. 31-33; salvage job, pp. 33-34; put back to use for diving experiments in early 1930s, p. 40; rescue techniques developed during late 1930s could possibly have saved crew members' lives, pp. 74-75, 90

S-51, USS (SS-162)
   Salvage efforts by USS Falcon (ARS-2) after sinking in September 1925, pp. 16, 26; underwater burning and welding tested during salvage, p. 71

Salvage Work
   Badders encouraged to pursue salvage work in mid-1920s, p. 13; salvage ship sent to rescue of S-51 (SS-162) in September 1925 had no divers and little equipment, pp. 16-17; method of raising submarine, pp. 20-26; recommendations made for pontoon improvements after S-51 (SS-162) salvage, pp. 26-28; F-boat salvaged off Honolulu in 1914 by sweeping wires under it, pp. 28-29; S-4 (SS-108) salvage was repetition of S-51 job, pp. 33-34; See: Diving; Falcon

San Diego
   Football widespread among military and colleges in mid-1930s, pp. 69-70

Saunders, Commander Harold E., USN (USNA, 1912)
   As officer in charge of S-4 salvage operation in 1928, p. 33

Sculpin, USS (SS-191)
   On scene during sister submarine Squalus' disaster in May 1939, p. 83

Sealab
   Saturation pressure technique used to allow divers to stay at great depths for long periods of time, p. 93

Sharks
   Though present, not a problem to Navy divers in Far East in early 1930s, pp. 51, 93

Sibitsky, Boatswain's Mate Second Class Martin C., USN
   Role in Squalus (SS-192) rescue in May 1939, p. 84

Snakes
   Badders has brush with poisonous coral snakes during night dive in Mariveles Bay in early 1930s, pp. 46-47

Somoza, Anastasio
   Nicaraguan President rewards Badders for his part in raising his sunken yacht in the mid-1940s, pp. 148-150; Badders's assessment of Somoza, pp. 150-152

Somoza Debayle, General Anastasio (USMA, 1946)
   Unfavorable assessment of Nicaraguan President in the late 1960s, pp. 148, 151-152

Soybeans
   Gas produced by these beans in hold of burning ship at Panama in the mid-1940s creates potentially explosive situation, pp. 145-146

Squalus, USS (SS-192)
   Use of pontoons in mid-1939 salvage operation, pp. 28, 89; rescue of 33 crew members using McCann chamber, pp. 43, 82-90; divers rush to scene of disaster, pp. 81-83; salvage operation, pp. 99-100; paperwork on operation, pp. 101-102

Submarine Duty
   Reluctance of some submariners to cooperate with rescue drills in early 1930s, pp. 38-39

Submarine Rescue Vessels
   After going for too long with just the Falcon (ARS-2) Navy converts other ships to this mission in late 1920s, p. 37

Sullivan, Commander William A., USN
    As officer in charge of Lafayette (AP-53) salvage, diverts equipment to Panama after 1942 operation, pp. 109-110

Tibbals, Chief Gunner Clarence L., USN
    Experiments with helium and oxygen mixtures for diving in mid-1920s, p. 76

Uniforms
    Slipshod apparel aboard Falcon (ARS-4) in 1924, pp. 14-15

Victory Ships
    Poor quality of construction poses problems during World War II transits of Panama Canal, pp. 121-125

Welding--Underwater
    Underwater burning and welding tried in S-51 (SS-162) salvage in mid-1920s, p. 71; explanation of, pp. 72-73; efficiency of welding in Panama Canal during World War II, pp. 73-74; equipment and technique developments in 1940s, pp. 74-75

Williams, Ted
    Holland (AS-3) baseball team plays Williams's high school team in San Diego in the mid-1930s, p. 68

Wisconsin, USS (BB-9)
    Badders fudges on forms and is sent to engine room instead of shoveling coal in 1918, pp. 2-3; patrols Atlantic during World War I, pp. 3-4